GROW

GROW

Fill your world with plants

Robyn Booth

Illustrated by Patti Blau

National Trust

Published by National Trust Books
An imprint of HarperCollins Publishers
1 London Bridge Street, London SE1 9GF
www.harpercollins.co.uk

HarperCollins Publishers
Macken House, 39/40 Mayor Street Upper, Dublin 1, D01 C9W8, Ireland

First published 2023

© National Trust Books 2023
Text © Robyn Booth 2023
Illustrations © Patti Blau 2023

ISBN 978-0-00-859523-4

10 9 8 7 6 5 4 3 2 1

The contents of this publication are believed correct at the time of printing.
Nevertheless, the publisher can accept no responsibility for errors or
omissions, changes in the detail given or for any expense or loss
thereby caused.

A catalogue record for this book is available from the British Library.

Printed and bound in Latvia

If you would like to comment on any aspect of this book, please contact us at
the above address or national.trust@harpercollins.co.uk

National Trust publications are available at National Trust shops or online at
nationaltrustbooks. co.uk

This book is produced from independently certified FSC™ paper
to ensure responsible forest management.

For more information visit: www.harpercollins.co.uk/green

Contents

Introduction   6

1. How to Start   8

2. Texture and Colour   30

3. Plants for Happiness and Healing   56

4. Cut Flowers   80

5. Indoor Plants   102

6. Grow Your Own   126

7. Greener Gardening   148

8. Plant Clinic   170

Glossary   186

Index   188

Picture Credits   192

Introduction

'The love of gardening is a seed once sown that never dies.'

Gertrude Jekyll

Why grow? Perhaps a better question is why wouldn't you? More of us than ever before are trying to balance busy, stressful lives with the need to take time out for ourselves once in a while. Gardening and being around plants is the perfect antidote to the hectic world outside, and once you've started there really is no going back.

Growing something, whether that be sowing seed, nurturing a veg patch or tending to houseplants, is the opportunity for you to take some time back for yourself. Experimenting and having fun with plants in your space, whether that is indoors or out, is an amazing way to turn off the 'noise' in your brain and focus on something deeply calming and satisfying.

As well as practising self-care, getting into gardening is a brilliant way to improve the environment around you. This book will show you the best plants to encourage wildlife into your space, meaning you not only get to marvel at the bees, butterflies and ladybirds you'll attract, but also at how much happier and healthier your greened-up world will be.

You don't need a garden to be a gardener. Just being near plants can help reduce stress levels, increase focus and reduce fatigue. That means bookcases, tabletops, desks and shelves can all be used to create your own green oasis, giving you the chance to express your creativity and style just as easily indoors as out.

If you're new to gardening and are not sure where to start, this book is here to help. Each chapter will cover the basics to get you going, no matter how much or how little space you have. Packed

with ideas and inspiration, from how to get the most out of your outdoor area, to choosing the perfect plant for each room in your home, there is everything you need to get started.

What is the number one thing you really need to remember when getting into gardening? Just have fun! Experiment, play with colour, texture and different techniques. You'll learn just as much from the things that don't quite go to plan as those that do. Whatever you like to grow, you'll be doing one of the best activities there is to support your mental and physical health, so grab those seeds, pick up the watering can and let's grow!

1. How to Start

Wondering where to begin with plants can be daunting. There is so much choice and so many varieties available it can be tempting to just pick one of everything and hope for the best. However, with a little planning and careful observation you will be able to maximise the potential of the space you have, avoid wasting money and grow plants that thrive. Whether you have a window box, a small plot or a bookshelf, here's how to get started.

What have you got?

Growing plants is thrilling stuff, and while you'd be forgiven for just diving straight in, it's worth taking a moment or two to step back and assess what you have.

The new garden

If you're in the exciting position of having your own home with a garden, you may want to wait a year to get to know your plot. This will give you the chance to decide how to tackle any pre-existing planting such as overgrown or mature shrubs and trees, see what comes up in any borders, or just get to know where the sunny, shady (and frosty) spots are.

If you're renting and not able to do too much to any garden space, it's still worth taking the time to note which are your sunny or shady areas. This will help you pick suitable plants for containers, which you can then take with you if you move.

Gardens in the sky

A beautiful balcony or window box can give you so much joy throughout the year. In a smaller space your plant selection is even more important, so you can make an impact in every season. As well as thinking about sun and shade, take note of how windy or sheltered your space is. Some plants will tough it out in an exposed spot, while others will struggle to thrive if they're battered by wind all year round.

Indoors

Thinking about your space isn't just limited to the outdoors. Light, heating, draughts and humidity levels all have a role in determining how successful your indoor plants will be. Be honest with yourself about how much time you are prepared to spend on taking care of them – and how likely you are to remember any watering. If you like, skip ahead to Chapter 5 which is all about houseplants.

Understanding soil

Plants thrive best in conditions they enjoy, so by getting to know what kind of soil you have you are much more likely to have a happy and healthy garden. It's really important to work with what you have. In the long run, this will avoid wasting a lot of time and money on plants that will struggle in unsuitable conditions.

TYPES OF SOIL

The texture of the soil and how it's held together will affect how much water it can retain, and in turn how fertile it will be. Most soils contain a certain amount of sand and clay, but the proportion of each can affect what type of plants will be best suited to your site.

Sandy

- These are soils that contain more sand and are likely to be free draining.
- This means less water is available to your plants, and the nutrients they need can be washed away.
- They are lighter and easier to dig.
- When rubbed between your fingers, sandy soil feels gritty and isn't easily rolled into a ball.

Clay

- Clay soils hold water and nutrients well.
- They can be prone to waterlogging and cracking.
- They are heavier and harder work to cultivate.
- Clay soil feels smooth, sticky and can easily be moulded into a ball or sausage.

Take a few soil samples from different areas of your garden and roll them between your fingers – this will give you a basic idea of the type of soil you have.

Sandy soil (middle) isn't easily rolled into a ball, whereas clay soil (bottom) can easily be moulded.

WHAT IS PEAT?

- Peat comes from peat bogs and is made up of partially decayed organic matter. It takes a long time to form, usually in waterlogged, acidic conditions.

- For many years peat has been sold in bags of potting compost and has been valued by gardeners for its ability to hold on to moisture and nutrients.

- However, peat bogs are a hugely valuable natural resource. They store massive amounts of carbon, are a vital ecosystem for plants, birds and insects, and also act as a natural flood defence. Unfortunately, in the UK we've lost around 80 per cent of our peat bogs. It takes about a year for 1mm (½sin) of peat to form, so restoring these precious areas takes an extremely long time.

- You can usually buy peat-free alternatives at your local garden centre. Check the labels carefully and avoid peat or 'reduced peat' products.

ROOM FOR IMPROVEMENT

All soils can benefit from adding organic matter. This can be in the form of well-rotted manure, composted green waste or homemade garden compost.

Adding organic matter will improve the structure of your soil. This means sandy soils can hold on to water and nutrients more easily, and the drainage of heavier clay will be improved.

Organic matter can be dug into the first 30cm (12in) or so of soil. An easier way to incorporate it is as a mulch – this simply means spreading a layer 5–7.5cm (2–3in) thick over the surface.

A STICKY SITUATION …

If you have heavy clay soil, a yearly mulch of garden compost will help with aeration and improve its drainage over time.

Avoid planting anything in clay soils until late winter or early spring. Try to break up the base of your planting hole to avoid water collecting in the bottom and waterlogging your plants.

It's always best to work with what you have rather than fighting against it, so why not try these suggestions for plants that don't mind a heavier soil.

- Japanese maple (*Acer japonicum/ A. palmatum*)
- Crab apple (*Malus spp.*)
- Rowan (*Sorbus spp.*)
- Buddleia
- Viburnum
- Fuchsia
- Hardy geraniums
- Hellebores
- Astrantias (shown above)

Aspect

Knowing the direction your garden faces and the amount of sunlight it receives each day is another way to make sure you make good plant choices. Some plants will enjoy being bathed in sunshine, while others will thrive in cooler, shadier spots.

South
- Sunny for most of the day in summer.
- Optimum growing conditions for many flowering plants, fruit and vegetables.
- Soil may dry out quickly with the need for additional watering during dry spells.

North
- Shady and cool.
- An excellent spot for architectural foliage and some flowering plants.
- Place any trees or shrubs at the end of the garden to avoid creating more shade.

East
- Sunny until late afternoon in summer.
- Suitable for foliage and many flowering plants that enjoy partial shade.
- Some spots of the garden will be sunnier for longer – grow your sun-lovers there.

West
- Sunny from late morning to evening in summer.
- Ideal for plants that like full sun or partial shade.
- Sun-loving plants and fruit trees will be happy in the brightest spots.

Buying plants

Spring and autumn are the best times to buy plants, as the soil is warm and moist enough for your new purchases to establish well.

Large garden centres do have extensive selections and may be able to offer certain plants more cheaply. However, independent growers and local nurseries are often experts in growing particular types of plants and will be able to give advice on what to pick, especially if you are looking for something specific.

Whichever option you choose, these tips will help you make the most of your available budget and avoid expensive mistakes.

PLANT-BUYING GUIDE

Make a plan Think about where the plant is going to go. What soil type do you have? What are the light conditions? How much space is there? This will help you determine not only the type of plants you go for, but how many.

Overall health and appearance Is the plant looking perky with plenty of new growth? Leaves that are turning yellow or brown could just be a sign the plant is hungry or in need of a good drink, but it could be a sign of disease. Some of these you can remedy at home but bear in mind that a plant that has been stressed may be weaker, more susceptible to pests and take longer to become established.

Pot bound This means the plant's roots have filled the pot and now have nowhere else to go but round and round. If this happens for a prolonged

period of time the plant may begin to get stressed from not being able to absorb enough water and nutrients. If you are buying something that has been in a pot for a long time, be sure to water it in well after planting. You may want to loosen the roots at the bottom of the root ball to encourage them to settle in more quickly.

Pests Check for signs of any insects on the foliage or flowers; you want to avoid bringing any unwanted visitors home with you.

Buds not blooms When buying a flowering plant, one with plenty of buds ready to open is better than one in full flower, however tempting it may look. This means you will be able to enjoy those flowers at home, rather than the best of the display having been spent at the garden centre.

Size Don't be put off by a smaller plant. While larger, more mature ones give instant impact, a smaller plant will not only be less expensive, but will get going more quickly and easily than you think.

Buy local Buying locally or UK grown plants is the best way to avoid the spread of pests and diseases that may be found on plants imported from abroad.

How to plant

You've got your plant home, you've picked the perfect spot – but what should you do with it now? Following these tried and tested methods will help get your plant off to a good start and, most importantly, improve its chances of survival.

GETTING READY

Container-grown plants can usually be planted at any time of year, unless the ground is frozen or waterlogged. Otherwise, spring or autumn are the best times to get plants settled in.

Make sure there are no perennial weeds such as nettles and docks in the space you want to plant into. You can use a hoe or hand fork to remove any smaller weeds.

REUSE AND RECYCLE

- Old compost bags come in useful for all sorts of things, including helping to suppress weeds.

- Lay them over the surface of your planting area and peg with metal ground staples or weigh down with bricks.

- You can also use them to transport any garden rubbish or in place of a trug when you're weeding.

You will need
- Spade or trowel
- Organic matter for mulching
- Bucket
- Up to 1 hour

SHRUBS AND PERENNIALS

1 Give your plant a good soak with a watering can or stand it in its container in a bucket of water. Allow to drain afterwards.
2 Dig a hole twice as wide and a little deeper than the container your plant is in.
3 Place the plant in the hole and check it will be at the same depth when planted as it is in its pot.
4 Remove the plant from its pot, place it in position and refill around the root ball. Firm in gently with your hands to ensure the roots are making good contact with the soil.
5 Water in well.
6 Mulch the surface of the soil after planting. This will help to retain the moisture you've just added by watering and suppress weeds for a time.

TREES

1 Water the tree before planting.
2 Remove its container or wrapping and tease out the roots at the bottom carefully.
3 Dig a hole the same depth and three times as wide as the root ball.
4 Place the tree in the hole, ensuring the spot where the roots start to flare out from the trunk is near the surface.
5 Refill around the root ball and firm in the soil.
6 Water in well.
7 Bare root trees can be planted in the same way, but backfill around the roots in stages so that large air pockets are removed. You want the roots to be making good contact with the soil so they can take up moisture and nutrients.
8 Small trees can be staked vertically. For larger trees, drive a stake into the ground at 45 degrees and attach to the tree using a tree tie.
9 After planting, apply a mulch annually and water regularly for the first couple of years. Check and loosen tree ties as necessary.
10 Remove the stake after four or five years.

Sowing seeds

Loo roll tubes are ideal for growing plants with long roots, such as climbing French beans.

Seeds are generally available to buy all year round and are a much more affordable way to get started than buying mature plants. They do require time and a little bit of space, but nothing beats the feeling of having nurtured something into being all by yourself.

Don't worry if you don't have access to a greenhouse – a windowsill can be a useful spot to get seeds going. Small, heated propagators are inexpensive and can help speed up germination, so are well worth a try. The following simple steps are especially suitable for half hardy plants like zinnias, cosmos and nicotiana that need a bit of warmth and protection to get going.

1 It may sound obvious, but reading the instructions on the packet is your best guide for when to sow, how deep, when to plant out and what kind of light conditions your plant will prefer.

2 Fill a clean seed tray or small pot with peat-free compost (multipurpose will work fine, or you can use seed compost if you have it).

3 Soak the seed tray or pot in water – you'll know it's moist enough when the surface of the compost darkens and appears to glisten.

4 Sprinkle seeds thinly on the surface of the compost. Check the packet for the required depth and cover the seeds with sifted compost to that depth. Larger seeds can simply be pushed in to the required depth before covering.

5 Label your tray or pot and put inside your propagator or place on your windowsill.

6 Keep the compost damp (not wet). If the compost still feels moist then don't add any more water. If you're using a propagator, remove the lid once seedlings emerge.

7 Once your seedlings have a few leaves, you can pot them on individually into modular trays or small pots. Tools called 'dibbers' are available to help gently tease out seedlings and separate them so you can pot them up, but you can just as easily use a pencil.

8 To remove your seedlings, insert your dibber or pencil into the compost and push up gently so the seedling loosens and comes away. Hold your seedling by its leaves as you carefully remove it.

9 Plant one seedling per module or pot. Push your dibber or pencil into the compost to make a hole and insert your seedling into it, pushing the compost back around the root firmly but gently. Make sure it's planted deep enough so that the first set of leaves is resting on the surface of the compost. This will help stop your seedling from getting weak and leggy.

SOWING SEEDS OUTDOORS

Another easy way to sow seeds is by putting them straight into the ground when it's warm enough; this is also known as 'direct sowing'. This is best done from about April onwards and is an ideal method for growing your hardier seeds (such as pot marigolds, poppies and cornflowers).

- You can sow your seeds straight into compost in raised beds, window boxes or pots of compost on your balcony. Remember to keep your seedlings moist by watering gently (use a watering can with a rose) if the weather is dry.

- If you've got room to grow outside in beds, take the time to prepare your soil first. Remove any weeds and rake over to make a fine, crumbly texture. This will make it easier for your seeds to get going if they're not having to battle against big clods of heavy, sticky soil.

- Sowing seed in straight lines into something called a 'drill' is an easy way to help distinguish your seedlings from any weeds that might also start to appear. To make a drill, use the end of a trowel or bamboo cane to mark out a shallow channel 1cm (½in) deep. Water this channel before sowing.

- You'll need to sow your seed thinly (so the seedlings don't become too crowded). Take a few at a time from the packet if they're large enough to handle, or if they're very tiny, pour them into your palm and sprinkle them a pinch at a time.

- Gently draw the soil back over the seed so it's covered – one way to do this is by pinching the soil on either side of your drill.

- At some point once the seedlings have appeared, you'll need to be brutal and pull some of them out: a process known as 'thinning out'. It seems a shame after waiting for them to start growing, but if you don't do it there won't be enough space for your plants to grow successfully. Your seed packet will tell you what distance there should be between each mature plant.

TIPS AND TRICKS

- If you don't have a propagator to put your pots of seeds into, try an old freezer bag or the clear plastic bags for toiletries like those given out at airports.

- Pop the bag over your pot of sown seed and secure with an elastic band or tie it on with string.

- Covering the seeds in this way seals in humidity – this means the compost stays moist and encourages your seeds to germinate.

- Remove the bag once seedlings start to emerge.

Basic tools

There is a huge variety of garden tools available to suit every budget and taste. All you need to get started, however, is a simple selection that will do for most jobs in the garden. Here are a few no gardener should be without.

Gloves Some gardeners choose not to wear them, but they are useful for protecting your hands, and pretty much essential if you're pruning roses. Opt for a good-quality pair of multipurpose ones, which will see you through most tasks.

Secateurs Pruning, deadheading and cutting back are regular tasks, so secateurs will probably be one of your most-used tools. They often come in a range of sizes, so pick a pair that feels comfortable.

Hand fork These are extremely useful for breaking up stony or compacted soil when planting and are great for weeding too.

Hand trowel These can be used during planting, or for scooping compost when sowing seed or potting on.

Watering can Available in various sizes depending on your needs. Those used for house plants come in a range of colours and materials and can be beautifully decorative in their own right. A watering can with a rose attachment will help distribute water gently and evenly.

Spade Essential for digging and planting. Border spades are slightly smaller than digging spades and useful for working in a compact space.

Fork A garden fork is perfect for working through soil in veg plots and borders ready for planting. The back of the fork can be helpful for breaking up large clods before raking.

ADD IT TO YOUR WISH LIST …

Kneeler Whether you love it or hate it, these make the job of weeding more comfortable.

Trug Essentially a strong, lightweight plastic container with handles. A bucket will do, but a proper trug is more durable and useful for all sorts of jobs.

Hoe If you've got a large area to weed, this will save you time and means less bending down.

Ground rake Ideal for creating perfectly textured soil ready for seeds or spreading mulch.

Pruning saw Makes pruning trees and shrubs a doddle.

Loppers Ideal for thinning out branches on big shrubs or small trees.

2. Texture and Colour

This is the exciting part. Now you've considered a few fundamentals when assessing your space, it's time to experiment and have fun. Keeping a certain theme in mind, such as a favourite colour or style, can help you stay focused when choosing plants. Think about how you want to feel in your outdoor area, what you want to do in it and how much time you have to look after it.

Containers

Containers are a brilliant way to experiment, create an interesting focal point or even disguise something. They are also perfectly suited for displays on balconies or in window boxes.

If you're renting or limited as to what you're able to do with an outdoor area, container gardening is a great way to add colour, as well as something interesting and beautiful to look at. It's easy to change and portable too.

Plants in containers are completely reliant on you for their care, so be realistic with how much time you are able to spend on feeding, watering, deadheading and pest control.

MIND THE GAP

Leave a gap of about 2–3cm (about 1in) below the rim of the pot after planting to allow for watering.

HOW TO PICK A POT

Size Don't shy away from large pots if you have a small space. Many small containers dotted about can look cluttered and will need lots more watering. Larger containers don't dry out as quickly and could be the perfect home for some architectural planting to add height and drama. A mix of sizes can create an interesting look.

Materials Terracotta gives a warm and traditional look, and modern versions tend to be frost-proof (it should say on the label when you buy it). Water can evaporate from them quickly, however, meaning plants can dry out easily in summer. On a balcony or roof terrace, lightweight containers made from aluminium or resin are a better option.

Colour Containers are a fun way to introduce another layer of colour and texture into your space, particularly with houseplants. Sticking to a colour palette or theme will help make everything look coherent.

Drainage If the container you've bought doesn't already have drainage holes you will need to drill some in yourself. Three or four medium-sized holes spaced out over the bottom of the pot should do it. Adding broken pieces of terracotta pot or polystyrene over drainage holes will prevent any compost falling through and prevent them from getting blocked.

TIP-TOP POTS

Once you've planted up your containers, some regular aftercare will keep them looking good for months.

Water Watering is key, especially in dry and hot spells. You may need to water once or twice a day if it's very warm. Using a watering can or hose, fill the container to the brim, allow to drain away and then fill once more.

Food Like any living thing, plants get hungry; they'll show it by turning yellow and looking generally weak and sad. A liquid seaweed feed contains all the essential nutrients without being too rich and is great for veg too. Try to top dress your pots each year with a fresh layer of compost to keep plants healthy.

Deadheading Remove any fading or dead flower heads as soon as possible. Cut back to a new bud or a new shoot lower down the plant. This will keep the plant's energy focused on making more flowers.

SUPER SUCCULENTS

Succulent bowls are incredibly easy to make and care for, and will reward you by looking fabulous all year round. Sempervivums, Rosularia spp. and most sedums are hardy enough to stay outdoors all year and need minimal care and attention. If you're not sure if you have green fingers then just try these simple steps – you might surprise yourself.

1 First, select your container. Let your imagination run free with your choice of material but try to incorporate drainage holes and aim for a container around 10cm (4in) deep.

2 Next, choose your succulents. If you want them to stay outside all year, stick to combinations of hardy sempervivums and sedums. If you can offer some protection from frost, you could try echeverias and dwarf agave. Play around with how you want to arrange your succulents before planting them up.

3 Fill your container by about two-thirds with very well-drained compost. Adding lots of horticultural grit works well. Place your largest succulent in first, either in the centre or off to one side.

4 Add the rest of your plants, making sure all the roots are covered with compost. Succulents don't mind being planted close together, so try not to leave too many visible gaps.

5 Top dress with pumice or grit to create a smart finish.

6 Marvel at your handiwork and place somewhere bright and sunny.

Quick wins

If you're short on space and time, sometimes you just need a bright burst of something to lift your spirits and spruce up your plot. In this situation, annuals are a good option.

Annuals are plants that grow, flower and die all in one year. However, they're often easy to grow and if you deadhead regularly, they will provide you with colour all summer long.

Pot marigold Edible petals, perfect for pollinators and available in a range of shades from deep orange to peach and apricot; an absolute must for a quick splash of colour.

Cosmos Dwarf forms, such as the cherry pink 'Antiquity', will suit smaller spaces. Keep deadheading to encourage flowers well into autumn. 'Double Click Cranberries' is a taller variety that will give you masses of frothy crimson blooms until the first frosts.

Gazania Easy to grow but needs full sun for the flowers to open. 'Kiss Bronze' comes in brilliant orange and is guaranteed to bring a smile to your face.

Zinnia Useful for cut flowers and comes in a myriad of colours to suit every taste. 'Purple Prince' is an excellent variety that produces long-lasting, brilliantly hued flowers on sturdy stems that look amazing in a vase.

CLOCKWISE FROM TOP LEFT
Gazania; scabious; sage; sunflower.

Mexican sunflower Full sun is needed to get the best from this beautiful plant. If you have the right spot you'll be rewarded with sunset-orange, daisy-like flowers until the nights turn colder.

Scabious From pale blue to velvety purple-black, the pretty pincushion flowers of scabious are a great draw for bees and butterflies.

Sage Don't just think about the edible herb here. So many vibrant ornamental flowering plants come under the common name of sage (or *Salvia*). Try *Salvia farinacea* or *S. splendens* for rich purples and bright scarlets.

Amaranth Edible and attractive, with luxuriously trailing fluffy flower heads that look as striking in a pot as they do in a border.

Straw flower Also known as the everlasting flower, these come in a huge range of colours from subtle apricots to punchy reds and oranges. Once cut and dried, the flowers still hold their colour well and so are perfect for arrangements later in the year.

Sunflowers The ever-popular sunflower comes in a range of sizes. Dwarf varieties such as 'Ms Mars' would suit a small space. If you have a larger area, go big with 'Earthwalker.' Leave some flower heads to go to seed as these will be perfect for feeding hungry birds getting ready for winter.

PLUG PLANTS

You may not have the space or time to grow anything from seed, or you may have left it a bit too late in the year. This is where plug plants come in handy. Put simply, these are young plants, halfway between a seed and a mature plant, usually grown in modular trays.

Herbs, veg and annual bedding plants are often grown in this way, and can be bought cheaply online from a huge range of nurseries or your local garden centre.

Go for 'garden ready' ones if you need to fill a pot or container quickly and

---

HOW TO …

If you are wondering how to get your new baby plants out without squashing them, grab a pencil and push the module up gently from the bottom. This will ease out the plant in one piece.

easily. Don't forget, regular feeding and watering will ensure they look their best and last as long as possible. If you've got a window box outside, or space on a windowsill indoors, why not try some easy veg for your salads and stir-fries?

Trailing plants Ivy, lobelia and calibrachoa will add a decorative edge and a splash of colour to your pots.

Evergreen Use evergreen plants mixed with florals to give structure. Try ivy, euonymus or herbs like rosemary, sage or thyme for fragrance and a long-lasting display.

Edibles Chillies, peppers and some tomato varieties are perfect for pots and easy to get hold of as plugs. Try basil and coriander on a bright windowsill.

AMAZING AMARANTH

- Amaranth is one of the world's oldest crops; the Aztecs and Incas of Central and South America believed it had supernatural powers.

- The seeds from the plant are gluten-free and rich in protein. Flour made from amaranth can be used in baking bread or muffins, as well as for thickening sauces.

- The leaves are high in fibre and a brilliant alternative to spinach. When finely chopped they are perfect for adding to soups and stir-fries.

Perfect Perennials

If you have the space, time and budget for perennials – plants that will last for more than one season – they will help create an impact and save you money in the long run.

Because they last longer, perennials are also an environmentally friendly choice. If you want plants that will reward you with the minimum of fuss, here are some suggestions that will suit most plots.

Hoverfly on yarrow.

FLOWERING PERENNIALS

Hardy geraniums Often underrated, these plants are an excellent choice for someone who wants colour and interesting foliage, but isn't sure where to start. Saucer-shaped flowers range from the deepest maroon to violet blue and baby pink. Once the first flush of flowers has finished, cutting back the old leaves will reward you with fresh new growth and more blooms.

Echinacea Pretty, daisy-like flowers beloved by bees; the large brown cone in the centre will stand all through the winter where you can admire it sparkling with frost on a sunny winter's day. It tolerates most soils and won't flop over in windy or wet weather.

Yarrow If attracting wildlife is a priority then you must include some of this in your sunniest spot. The flat-topped flower heads are a great resting place

Hakon grass.

Choisya ternata.

and food source for butterflies, bees and hoverflies. 'Cassis' is a stunning wine-red variety that contrasts beautifully with its feathery green foliage.

Catmint Brush against this at the end of a long day and feel your stress melt away thanks to its wonderfully calming fragrance. Once it has finished flowering, cut back the old stems and enjoy another flush of lavender-blue blooms among grey-green foliage.

GRASSES

Hakon grass Also known as Japanese forest grass, this forms gently cascading mounds of soft green, which turns a beautiful bronze in autumn. Fully hardy

with airy flower heads in late summer, this plant really does have it all.

Carex These typically evergreen plants with their grass-like foliage are hardy, great for containers and have so much variety. From silvery grey to copper or acid-yellow, mix these among your flowers for a playful change in texture.

Fargesia Related to bamboo but better behaved, this will form beautifully architectural canes clothed in soft green leaves throughout the year. Fully hardy and excellent in a large pot, place in a sheltered corner to protect the leaves from being scorched by drying winds.

Fescues These fine-leaved grasses are extremely versatile and work in a wide range of planting schemes. Preferring full sun, *Festuca glauca* combines beautifully with the purple-blue spikes of salvias or the ghostly bark of birch trees.

SHRUBS

Viburnum Foliage, fruit and flowers can all be found on these wildlife-friendly shrubs. They can make quite large specimens and while they are not fussy about soil, they will appreciate a sheltered spot away from drying winds.

Cornus Another group of plants that offers a huge range of seasonal interest. Try *Cornus alba* 'Sibirica' for the brightest blood-red stems. A spot in full sun will really bring out the best colour in this lovely variety.

Choisya Unfussy and easy to grow, with glossy evergreen foliage and beautifully perfumed flowers reminiscent of orange blossom. Choisya is also great for bees due to its abundant nectar.

Fatsia Lending a lush, tropical feel to a space, fatsias have gloriously glossy, deep-green leaves and spherical, creamy white flowers in autumn. They combine well with grasses and bamboos, or you can simply use them as a focal point in a tricky shady corner.

GREEN AND THRIFTY

Most perennials are easily split up into smaller plants as they get bigger. This is a process called division. It looks brutal but be brave and you will have more plants to add to your plot, all for free.

1 Spring or autumn is the best time to try this as your new plants will be able to get going while the ground is moist.

2 Dig up your 'parent' plant and shake off the excess soil so you can see the roots.

3 Some plants can be pulled apart by hand to form smaller clumps that you can then re-plant. Plants with tougher roots may need to be cut into sections with a spade. Another technique is to use two garden forks pushed into the centre of the plant, back to back; then use them as levers to break it apart.

4 Make sure your divisions have visible, healthy-looking shoots and roots.

5 Re-plant somewhere new or pot them up to build up their size.

Reach for the sky

Climbers are a great way to add an extra layer of interest to your planting and soften or hide walls and fences. They can make your space appear bigger too by disguising boundaries.

Some will even thrive in containers provided they are well fed and watered throughout the summer months. Certain climbers need to be cut back at specific times of year in order to look their best and stay within the space you want to fill. It's well worth doing a bit of research online or checking the label for what to do and when so you get the best results year after year.

Unless it's self-clinging like ivy, your climber will need some support. Wigwams (shop-bought or made with bamboo canes or hazel sticks) look attractive and provide height, as well as being useful for growing annuals like sweet peas or morning glory. If you want a more permanent covering on a wall or fence, see How to Plant Climbers (page 47).

SEED STARTERS

- To grow annual climbers from seed and give them the best start, use the cardboard tubes from loo rolls.

- Fill these with peat-free multipurpose compost and sow your seeds to the correct depth.

- This method is perfect for sweet peas and runner beans or climbing French beans. Their roots will stay undisturbed and, if kept on a windowsill or other raised surface, away from the worst of the slugs and snails.

- Plant the whole lot in the ground when it's warm enough, and then enjoy.

You will need
- Spade and fork
- Organic matter
- Vine eyes
- Wire
- Bamboo canes (or similar)
- Up to 1 hour

HOW TO PLANT CLIMBERS

1 If you have a wooden fence or trellis, screw in little metal loops (vine eyes) 45cm (18in) apart and fix a length of wire horizontally between them. You may need two sets of these. A drill and rawl plugs will be useful if securing to a brick or stone wall.

2 Prepare the soil and planting hole as for perennials (see page 21), at least 30cm (12in) away from the support. Again, it's worth checking the needs of your specific climber; for example, clematis often likes to be planted deeper than other climbing plants.

3 Use bamboo canes (easily sourced online or recycle them from your own bamboo plant) as guides near your wall or fence. Insert three or four canes, evenly spaced, into the base of the planting hole and tie them to the wire at the top to hold them in place.

4 After planting, backfill with soil and firm it down.

5 Spread out the stems and tie them to the canes loosely with soft twine in a figure of eight.

6 Water in well and add a mulch, keeping it clear of the stems. Water regularly in its first year.

Think ahead

Bulbs are a brilliantly easy way to work some seasonal interest into your plot. There are bulbs to suit even the smallest of spaces, and a huge selection of colours and flower shapes to choose from. If you want to cheat a bit, buy potted bulbs in February or March. These are ready-sprouted and just need planting in the ground or your favourite container.

ABOVE AND OPPOSITE
Allium 'Purple Sensation';
tulips in contrasting colours.

Crocus Beautiful in pots or popping up en masse in a lawn or under trees. *Crocus minimus* 'Spring Beauty' has striking painterly splashes of deep purple against soft lilac petals.

Tulips Varieties can flower from early through to mid-spring and come in a dazzling array of heights, shapes and colours. Go tasteful with complementary shades or be playful with contrasting colours such as orange and purple.

Grape hyacinth These brilliant blue flower spikes are ideal in a shady spot or mixed in with other bulbs in pots for an extra layer of interest.

Allium From huge to dainty, with stunning spherical flower heads. 'Summer Drummer' is a tall and late-flowering variety.

Lily Scent, height and colour, lilies have it all. Full sun and well-drained soil or a

gritty compost mix in a pot will help you get the best from them. All parts are toxic to animals so exercise caution if you have pets.

Imperial fritillary Impressive height with an unusual flower-form in striking oranges and yellows. These will appreciate well-drained soil and full sun.

Narcissus Dwarf varieties are attractive in pots, while larger ones will look great under trees. Choose scented varieties for even more joy.

Dwarf iris Pops up to brighten the dullest late-winter days. These are perfect for pots and window boxes with decent drainage, and come in a range of colours, from cheery yellow, sky blue and imperial purple.

Snowdrops They are tougher than their delicate appearance may suggest and are easily divided to create more clumps that you can spread about. Copes well in shady spots.

BULB LASAGNE

Try this recipe for a spring display that will look perfect in pots.

1   Make sure your chosen container has a drainage hole and cover this with either a layer of grit or some broken pieces of pot.

2   Fill the pot about one-third full of compost.

3   Your latest-flowering and largest bulbs go at the bottom – in this recipe it's tulips. Cover them with compost.

4   Your middle layer comes next – these are your hyacinths and daffodils. Again, cover with compost.

5   Your final layer will be your smallest, earliest-flowering bulbs. Plant your grape hyacinths here and cover them with compost.

6   Your bulbs won't appear until spring, so you could add plug plants (ivy, violas, wallflowers, etc.) on top for a final layer that will look good through the winter until the bulbs appear.

You will need
- Tulip bulbs
- Daffodil bulbs
- Hyacinth bulbs
- Grape hyacinth bulbs
- Your bedding plant of choice
- Multipurpose peat-free compost
- Large container

HOW TO PLANT BULBS IN THE GROUND

Spring-flowering bulbs (tulips, daffodils, etc.) are planted in autumn, and summer-flowering ones (lilies, nerines, etc.) are planted in spring.

If you want naturalistic drifts of flowers, scatter the bulbs onto the surface of your soil. Then plant them where they land to twice their depth. Alternatively, if you'd rather have clumps of bulbs in certain areas, dig a wide hole to the appropriate depth and plant in a group before covering them back over.

Solutions for a shady spot

If you have a cool, shady garden or balcony, you can transform it from gloomy to glorious with just a few key plants.

While permanent deep shade is tricky, partial or dappled shade will allow suitable plants to flourish. Ferns are your friend in a garden like this, with their stunning textured foliage acting as a beautiful, mesmerising backdrop.

Don't think you have to forgo flowers in shade either – those adapted to woodland conditions will thrive. A productive patch is also within reach as lettuces, leafy greens and herbs will love the cooler growing conditions.

TOP TO BOTTOM
Ferns with lily of the valley; tulips; daffodils.

TEXTURE

Ferns If a beautiful backdrop to your bulbs and shade-tolerant flowers is what you're after, go for ferns. Create interest by mixing evergreen and deciduous types. Most like a bit of moisture but *Dryopteris filix-mas* will do well in drier conditions.

Grasses and sedges Forming well-behaved clumps that won't take over, these plants create a pleasing contrast next to broader-leaved specimens.

Plants with different colours in their leaves (known as variegated) can help brighten up a dark spot. *Carex oshimensis* 'Everest' works well in a container.

Foliage and stems Flowers aren't the only stars of the show. Think about the shape, size and colour of the foliage plants you might want to include. Heucheras, brunnera and bamboo are all great options for shade.

Grape hyacinths.

COLOUR

Balconies and window boxes
Shade-loving colourful plants that work well in containers are easy to find. Try cyclamen, dwarf hardy fuchsias or pretty spring bulbs such as daffodils and grape hyacinths.

Woodland garden If a few trees are casting shade on your plot in the summer months, a woodland-style garden may be the way forward. Bulbs will make the most of the light in early spring, and once summer approaches foxgloves, hardy geraniums and Turk's-cap lilies will fill the garden with colour.

City life Urban gardens are often warmer than those in more exposed areas, so you could try experimenting with impressive tree ferns, Chusan palms or hardy bananas.

FERN FACTS

- Ferns are one of the oldest plant species on Earth, growing even before the first appearance of dinosaurs.

- They don't reproduce through flowers or seeds, but instead make millions of tiny spores.

- Ferns don't have typical leaves either; instead they have branches that are fused together to make fronds.

- One of the world's largest ferns, *Dicksonia antarctica*, grows in the wild in Australia and Tasmania and can reach up to 15m (50ft) in height.

- Ferns do not always coexist happily with other plants. In the wild some species release toxic substances into the air that act as a herbicide. They do this to destroy other plants close to them and create more space for themselves.

BE PRODUCTIVE

Eat your greens Leafy salad crops, including mustard, mizuna, radicchio and rocket, will much prefer a cool, shady spot and are great in containers too. If you've got more space, try kale, chard and fennel.

Fruit There are plenty of fruit trees and bushes that have been developed specially for smaller spaces and container growing. Try your hand at redcurrants or blackberries for a taste of summer. If you have a large container, give rhubarb a go.

Herbs Various mints, marjoram, chives and parsley prefer some dappled shade and will also love life in a pot. They are beautifully decorative as well as edible.

3. Plants for Happiness and Healing

Studies have shown that just being around plants can have a positive effect on our sense of wellbeing. There's no doubt that time spent with growing things, whether indoors or out, is an excellent way to bring a feeling of calm and improve our mood. Here are some ideas on how to harness some of those benefits in your own space.

Scent

Smell is one of the most powerful senses, so it's not surprising that scent can play a big role in how we feel. Receptors in the nose send messages to the part of the brain that processes memory, mood and emotion. This means that filling your garden and home with scent is a simple way to lift your spirits, no matter what time of year it is.

Bergamot.

PLANTS FOR CALM

Bergamot Sometimes known as bee balm, bergamot has a soothing citrus scent and is perfect for making calming herbal teas. This hardy perennial has pinky-mauve flowers that are adored by pollinators, so you'll be doing good as well as feeling good if you include this somewhere in your plot.

Lavender Used since ancient times, lavender has a deserved reputation for being one of the most calming plants there is. The essential oils distilled from the flower spikes can reduce anxiety, blood pressure and heart rate. Lavender oil can be used for aromatherapy; breathe in the fragrance for at least three minutes to receive the most benefit.

Peppermint The attractive, fluffy purple flowers are another excellent nectar source for bees and the oil can be used in aromatherapy for reducing

SUPER STEMS – GINGER

You may well regard fresh ginger as a tropical spice that needs masses of heat in a greenhouse to grow well in the UK. However, proper fresh ginger is surprisingly easy to grow at home and can be added to all manner of dishes, including salads and salsas. Not only will it provide you with a delicious crop, but it will also make a rather lovely houseplant.

1 Head to your local supermarket and look for pieces of ginger root, as fresh as possible and ideally with 'eyes' (small yellow tips from where the shoots will sprout).

2 Plant the root pieces in a pot of well-drained compost, adding extra grit if needed (or use seed compost). Make sure the eyes are just level with the surface.

3 Place the pot in a propagator or cover with a clear plastic bag, keeping it in a warm and sunny spot (ideally at 20°C/68°F). Try to keep the compost damp but not too wet.

4 In a few weeks' time you'll start to notice green tips. Remove the bag and keep your plant somewhere warm and bright, watering occasionally.

5 After 6–8 months you can harvest your fresh ginger.

6 Carefully remove a bulbous looking root from the pot – it should be a soft yellow colour. This is the part you can use fresh by slicing thinly and adding to chicken or fish dishes for a crisp, warm hit of flavour.

stress. Peppermint teas can be useful for easing anxiety, or a few drops of oil applied to the temples for tension headache relief.

Hops Also a component of beer, this vigorous perennial climber contains bitter resins which have a sedative effect. The attractive cone-like flowers go papery in early autumn when they can be harvested. Hops can be ingested in a tea or used in a 'hop pillow' to aid sleep.

Chamomile This well-known plant, popularly used in teas, has many medicinal uses, including the treatment of skin conditions and colds. The scent is thought to affect receptors in the brain, helping you to switch off so you feel calm and ready for a good night's sleep.

SOOTHING SLEEP PILLOW

If you need something to help relieve stress and relax, try this simple sleep pillow for a restful night.

You will need
- 32g dried chamomile flowers
- 32g dried lavender buds
- 16g dried hops
- 2–3 drops lavender essential oil
- Drawstring bag, either muslin or any other soft fabric you prefer
- 15–20 minutes

1 Place all the herbs in a bowl and stir gently.

2 Add the essential oil and mix together.

3 Stuff your bag with the mixture, but not too tightly – if the herbs can move around, they'll be able to release more of their beneficial fragrance.

4 Pull the drawstrings tight and tie them together.

5 Tuck the bag into your pillowcase at bedtime.

PLANTS FOR A MOOD BOOST

Lemon balm In the same family as mint, lemon balm has a wonderfully uplifting citrus fragrance and is very easy to grow. Used in a tea, the dried leaves can help to stimulate focus and improve memory.

Ginger The same plant that produces root ginger (the fleshy rhizome available in supermarkets) can be grown at home and harvested fresh as 'stem' ginger. The warm, uplifting scent of sliced fresh ginger is the perfect pick-me-up for a gloomy winter day. Fresh ginger contains chemical compounds that when ingested, increase blood flow and boost your metabolism, both of which will help make you feel more energised.

Citrus Sweet orange and lemon essential oils have traditionally been thought to provide mood-elevating benefits, as well as helping with motivation. Try breathing in a few drops of essential oil or adding lemon juice to hot water to relieve nausea and heartburn.

Rosemary and basil These deliciously aromatic Mediterranean herbs have a punchy fragrance that stimulates the brain, boosting mood, focus and energy. To help stay alert during a long car journey, pop a fresh sprig of rosemary on your dashboard to squeeze and sniff occasionally, or try inhaling a few drops of basil essential oil.

FILL YOUR GARDEN WITH FRAGRANCE

There is a huge range of easy-to-grow garden plants that will fill your plot, large or small, with fragrance to lift your spirits. Adding a mix of perennials and climbers can help create delicious wafts of perfume at different points through the garden. For maximum enjoyment, focus on growing scented plants in areas you use most. This could be a seating area or doorway, or even cracks between paving stones in the path up to your front door.

TOP 10 PLANTS FOR SCENT

Rose This garden staple is famous for its perfume, ranging from heavy floral to scents reminiscent of sparkling wine. With climbers as well as compact bushes available in deep jewel tones or soft pastels, there is a rose for everyone.

Stocks Cottage garden favourites with flowers that emit a warm, spicy scent and come in a wide range of colours. They make a great cut flower, either fresh or dried. Best grown from seed and placed somewhere sunny and well drained.

DIY ROSEWATER

Rosewater has a long history of use in many parts of the world as a natural way to soothe the skin. Roses contain antiseptic properties that help heal wounds and, of course, a gorgeous fragrance that boosts mood and alleviates anxiety.

This simple recipe will give you rosewater that you can use in cooking, to soothe the skin or as a room mist to give your home a hint of floral freshness.

You will need
- 4–5 blossoms of fragrant roses
- Water
- Saucepan
- Glass bottle or jar
- 45 minutes

1   Remove the petals and rinse carefully to remove dust and any little insects.

2   Add the petals to a saucepan and just cover with water.

3   Over a medium–low heat, bring to a simmer and cover the pan with a lid.

4   Simmer for 20–30 minutes until the petals have lost most of their colour.

5   Strain the mixture into a container to separate the petals from the water.

6   Put your rosewater in a glass jar or bottle. If kept in the fridge it will last for around 3–4 months.

7   Add to cheesecakes, strawberry tarts and smoothies, or spritz onto the face for a skin refresh.

Honeysuckle.

Sweet alyssum.

Honeysuckle If you're looking for a plant with a heady perfume for warm evenings, then look no further. Honeysuckle is great for pollinators, and some varieties produce berries in autumn. Due to its vigorous climbing nature, honeysuckle is very useful for screening unsightly walls and fences quickly and will reward you with abundant flowers all summer long.

Sweet alyssum Forming a colourful mass of tiny flowers, this annual is easily grown from seed or bought as plug plants. It's also perfect for small pots, window boxes and windowsills. If you have any aphids lurking, this is good for attracting hoverflies, which will feast on

them with no need for nasty chemical insecticides.

Star jasmine (*Trachelospermum jasminoides*) This heavenly scented evergreen climber will benefit from a sheltered sunny spot, but also copes well in partial shade. As it's slow growing it suits a smaller space and is well worth planting near your outdoor seating area so you can get the most from its sweet, floral perfume.

Sweet peas These reliable annuals are easy to grow from seed and make excellent cut flowers, particularly if you opt for a longer-stemmed variety. The traditional variety 'Cupani' is hard to beat

Chocolate cosmos.

Mahonia.

for scent and colour, so if you only have room for one make it this.

Chocolate cosmos With a distinct milk-chocolate aroma, this variety is easy to grow from seed and you will be rewarded with velvety, bowl-shaped red-brown flowers in late summer. If you have somewhere to keep it free from frost then it will come back the following year.

Clematis As well as a profusion of flowers, some varieties of clematis are noted for their scent, particularly *Clematis armandii* 'Snowdrift'. With masses of almond-scented flowers in March and April, this plant will give you a warm,

happy feeling when lots of other things in the garden have yet to get going.

Mahonia This provides architectural interest and acid-yellow flowers with a beautiful lily-of-the-valley fragrance. Often with glossy evergreen foliage, it is ideal for a shady spot.

Heliotrope If you are fond of warm, creamy fragrances with a hint of vanilla, then make space for heliotrope somewhere in your garden. Happy in a pot or in a border, enjoy clusters of tiny flowers in lilac or deep purple that really pack a punch with scent. You may need to bring it indoors for some winter protection if you live in a cold area.

Home remedies

There are many everyday ailments that can affect us all from time to time. Some of these have been treated with plant-based remedies since ancient times. Below are some simple ways to use home-grown plants that can help make you feel better and relieve bumps and scrapes, headaches and colds. If symptoms persist, however, don't delay in seeking medical advice.

COUGHS AND COLDS

What? Garlic, ginger, fresh lemon juice.

Why? The above ingredients are thought to have some antibacterial and antiviral properties, helping to relieve symptoms.

How to use Add some grated ginger and two cloves of crushed garlic to boiling water. Allow to simmer for 1–2 minutes and add the juice from a fresh lemon. Strain the mixture and allow to cool a little before drinking.

A WORD TO THE WISE

If you are taking medication, are pregnant, breastfeeding or about to undergo surgery, then speak to your doctor or pharmacist for advice before trying any plant-based remedies.

NAUSEA

What? Peppermint, ginger.

Why? The leaves and the oil extracted from peppermint are thought to have a calming effect on the stomach, helping food digest more easily.

Ginger contains a naturally occurring chemical that affects the digestive and central nervous system, alleviating nausea.

How to use Boil 500ml of water and add 15–20 fresh peppermint leaves. Turn off the heat and let the leaves steep in the water for 10–15 minutes. Strain the leaves and serve warm.

In addition, eating ginger biscuits, adding the fresh root when cooking, or chewing on candied ginger can also help relieve nausea.

PICK-ME-UP PARSLEY

- If your headache is 'self-inflicted', parsley tea makes an excellent hangover cure.

- Add a handful of finely chopped fresh parsley leaves to boiling water, leave for a few minutes then strain.

- Parsley is rich in iron, vitamins and minerals, and ideal to help you feel rejuvenated and refreshed.

HEADACHES

What? Basil, rosemary.

Why? If basil and rosemary are used fresh, these Mediterranean herbs are said to help stimulate the body's natural processes and relieve pain.

How to use Chewing fresh basil leaves is simple and effective and can also freshen the breath. Inhale the steam after boiling basil and rosemary together or allow both herbs to soak in boiled water for a few minutes, strain and drink warm.

TROUBLE SLEEPING

What? Chamomile.

Why? Chamomile has mild sedative properties; it relaxes muscles and acts as an anti-inflammatory.

How to use Best ingested as a tea. Use 2 teaspoons of dried chamomile for 250ml of water and simmer for a few minutes. Use honey if desired to add sweetness.

MAGIC MOUTHWASH

The brilliant oranges, yellows and reds of nasturtium flowers give a splash of colour to a salad, while its leaves add the perfect peppery crunch.

However, did you know that nasturtiums also have antibacterial properties? Chewing on the flowers and leaves not only acts as a natural mouth cleanser, but the distinctive pepper taste helps stimulate the appetite.

CUTS AND SCRAPES

What? Aloe vera.

Why? The soothing, gel-like substance within the leaves of the aloe vera plant is rich in antioxidants and minerals, which helps to speed up wound healing.

How to use If you have an aloe plant on your windowsill, cut a piece of leaf, squeeze out the gel from inside and apply directly to your skin. Alternatively, a bottle of aloe vera gel can be bought from most supermarkets, chemists or health food shops.

ANXIETY

What? Lavender.

Why? The essential oils in lavender have a calming effect without making you feel too sleepy, ideal for when you need to be calm and in control.

How to use Apply the essential oil on your pulse points or apply a few drops onto a tissue and inhale deeply for a few minutes.

ANCIENT ALOE

A papyrus scroll dating back to 1500 BC, known as the Ebers Papyrus, records many remedies used by the ancient Egyptians.

Although some of the advice is questionable by modern standards, it does encourage the use of aloe vera for treating burns and ulcers, which is still supported by science today.

Cocktails and mocktails

With these simple recipes, you can pop a few sprigs of something home-grown into your own plant-based pick-me-up. Then just sit back and relax.

MINTY SUMMER SPRITZ

You will need
- Handful of fresh mint
- 25ml vodka (optional)
- 1 tbsp sugar syrup
- 1 tbsp lemon (or lime juice)
- Lemonade

1   Pick a handful of fresh mint leaves and put in a cocktail shaker (or a travel coffee cup if you don't have a shaker).

2   Add a handful of ice and add the vodka (if using), sugar syrup and lemon or lime juice. Shake well.

3   Pour into a tall glass and top up with lemonade.

ROSE SANGRIA

You will need
- 10 fresh strawberries, chopped
- 1 fresh orange, chopped
- 1 tbsp sugar syrup
- 125ml rosé wine
- 5–10 slices of lemon
- Handful of fragrant rose petals
- Sparkling water or lemonade

1 Mix the chopped fruit with the sugar syrup and leave for 20 minutes. This will help the fruit flavour mix more easily into the wine.

2 Add the rosé, lemon slices and rose petals.

3 Leave in the fridge for 1–2 hours.

4 After refrigerating, add some ice to a glass and pour in the sangria. Top up with sparkling water or lemonade for some refreshing bubbles!

LAVENDER MARTINI

You will need
- 200g sugar
- 1 tbsp dried lavender buds
- 25ml vodka
- 1 tbsp lemon juice
- 1 tbsp sugar syrup
- Lemon slices to serve

1 First make the lavender syrup. Boil 250ml of water and 200g of sugar together until the sugar dissolves. Remove from the heat and add the dried lavender buds. Infuse for 20 minutes, strain and allow to cool.

2 Fill your cocktail shaker with ice, add the vodka, lemon juice, ½ tablespoon of lavender syrup and the sugar syrup. Shake well.

3 Strain into a martini glass and garnish with a slice of lemon

ROSEMARY AND ORANGE REFRESHER

You will need
- 2 sprigs of rosemary
- 3–4 slices of fresh orange, plus extra for serving
- 50ml gin
- 1 tbsp sugar syrup
- Tonic water or lemonade

1 Pull the leaves off one sprig of rosemary and chop finely.

2 Blend chopped rosemary and orange slices together in a mixer or macerate in a bowl.

3 Add the orange and rosemary mix to your shaker. Add the gin and sugar syrup and shake well.

4 Strain the mixture and pour into your glass; top up with tonic water or lemonade. Add a sprig of rosemary and a slice of orange to serve.

GRAPEFRUIT AND GINGER SPRITZER

You will need
- 1 grapefruit; reserve some slices for serving
- 3 cans of ginger ale
- 1 tbsp sugar syrup
- Handful of fresh basil

1 Juice the grapefruit.

2 Half-fill a pitcher with ice and add the grapefruit juice, ginger ale and sugar syrup.

3 Stir well.

4 Add the fresh basil and stir again.

5 Serve in a tall glass with a slice of grapefruit.

THYME LEMONADE

You will need
- 2.2kg sugar
- 1 bunch of fresh thyme; reserve some sprigs for serving
- Juice of 10 lemons

1 In a saucepan, bring the sugar, thyme and 250ml of water to a boil, stirring until the sugar is dissolved.

2 Stir in the lemon juice and add 1.5 litres of cold water.

3 Strain into a pitcher and refrigerate for at least 1 hour.

4 Serve over ice and garnish with sprigs of thyme.

RASPBERRY ROSE FIZZ

You will need
- 100g sugar
- 15–20 fresh raspberries
- 1 tbsp lemon juice
- 1 tsp of rosewater
- Tonic water or lemonade
- Rose petals (for garnish)

1   First make the raspberry syrup. Boil 125ml of water with 100g of sugar until the sugar is dissolved. Once cool, add the fresh raspberries, mash to a pulp and then strain. You can bottle any leftovers and add to desserts or other drinks.

2   Add the lemon juice, 1 tbsp raspberry syrup and the rosewater to a shaker, together with some ice, and shake well.

3   Strain the contents of your shaker into your glass. Add ice and tonic water or lemonade and decorate with rose petals.

MINT LIMEADE

You will need
- 1 cucumber, peeled and roughly chopped
- Handful of fresh mint leaves, plus extra to serve
- Juice of 2 limes, plus lime wedges to serve
- 50g sugar

1   Add the cucumber and mint leaves to a blender, together with the lime juice and sugar.

2   Blitz on a high speed until everything is nicely blended.

3   Serve immediately over ice, garnished with a wedge of lime and a sprig of mint.

Winter wonder

There's no doubt that the winter months can have their own beauty. There can be glittering frosts, pristine blankets of snow and sometimes a bright, fresh day that is perfect for a walk. The drawbacks, however, are fewer hours of daylight, colder temperatures and lots of cloud. This combination of factors can affect our mood and energy levels, as well as our sleeping and eating habits.

There are ways to make winter less dreary though. Many plants can provide a bit of cheer by offering scent, texture and colour, so why not aim to include one or two in your plot to give you a mood boost when you need it most? Doing something physical in nature is a great way to support your mental health and if you do have a garden, whatever its size, you'll be tempted to go out and enjoy it whatever the weather.

TOP 10 PLANTS FOR WINTER INTEREST

Wintersweet This beautiful large shrub or small tree has the most deliciously perfumed pale-yellow flowers. Flowering from January, the branches are perfect for understated flower arrangements.

Hellebores The common name of Christmas rose is somewhat misleading as hellebores rarely flower at Christmas, but in January and February expect a treat as the saucer-shaped flowers appear. Try *Helleborus x ericsmithii* 'Ivory Prince' for creamy green blooms flushed with a wash of pink, perfect for brightening a shady spot.

DIY BIRD FEEDER

Lots of small birds can use a helping hand in winter, so here's how to make a tasty treat to keep them going on the coldest of days.

You will need
- 1 block of lard
- Pine cone
- String
- A mix of seeds, nuts and dried fruit, such as raisins and cranberries; you can buy this ready-made or make your own mix
- 20–30 minutes

1. Warm the lard gently by placing on top of a radiator for a few minutes.

2. While the lard is softening, tie some string onto the top of a pine cone, making a loop so it can be hung up outside.

3. Once the lard is nice and soft, tip it into a mixing bowl and add your seed, nut and fruit mix.

4. Stir until well mixed together.

5. Press handfuls of the lard mixture onto the pine cone until it is completely covered.

Snowdrops Snowdrops have a delicate appearance that belies their tough nature. Often the first plants of the year to flower, they're perfect for planting in drifts under trees or wherever you have shade. The white petals will shine brightly, even on a dull day.

Cyclamen Another tough plant, cyclamen can tolerate dry shade, a big ask for most plants. They also look great planted under trees. Rich purples, soft pinks and bright whites will provide you with colour from late winter to early spring. Give them an annual mulch to protect from drying out in summer and the worst of the winter cold.

Cornus Plant in full sun to really get the glow from the bare stems of these beautiful shrubs. Try *Cornus sanguinea* 'Midwinter Fire' for a warming blaze of orange and yellow.

Tibetan cherry If you have a sheltered, sunny spot and some space to fill, consider adding this small tree. Its glossy, coppery bark is the star of the show, adding beautiful texture to any planting scheme. White, bowl-shaped flowers in spring and buttery yellow autumn colour means you won't be disappointed in any season.

Christmas box If you like evergreens, then this hardy winter-flowering shrub

HAPPY HOLLY

Holly was treated with great respect by the ancient inhabitants of Northern Europe, believing that it was a home for fairies and spirits. By medieval times, it was thought (somewhat optimistically) that drinking ale under a holly tree would let you consume as much as possible, with no ill-effects.

is a must. It adores shade and would be ideal for a woodland border. Scented, pure white blooms contrast beautifully with dark, glossy green leaves. Try planting near a path or door so you can enjoy a waft of scent every time you brush past it.

Viburnum Try *Viburnum x bodnantense* 'Dawn' for clusters of sweetly scented rose pink or soft white flowers on bare stems. This is a sizeable shrub, so it needs some space but tolerates most soils. It will do well in full sun or partial shade.

4. Cut Flowers

What is a cut flower? Any flower that is picked fresh and used for decorative arrangements can be described as a cut flower. Growing, picking and arranging your own blooms is incredibly satisfying. In an instant you have a perfect gift for a friend, or a bright pop of colour on the kitchen table to cheer you up.

You may have room for a dedicated cut flower patch, but if not, there are plenty of options for growing in containers. The main thing is to experiment and have fun. If things don't go to plan, or you don't like a colour combination, you can just start again. Don't be afraid to make mistakes – you'll learn a lot and it will be all the more rewarding when you find a magical combination of colours and textures you love.

How to create a cut flower patch

There are three things to consider when planting a cut flower patch: what, how and where.

WHAT TO GROW

• To get the most out of your patch, try a combination of annuals, biennials and a few perennials.

• You can have flowers even earlier in the year by adding bulbs like daffodils, hyacinths, tulips or alliums. Although these won't continue to produce flowers once picked, they'll give you a splash of spring colour.

HOW TO GROW

• If you want to create a dedicated cutting patch, it's best to grow your cut flowers in rows, in beds no more than 1m (3¼ft) wide. It's much easier to cut your blooms if you can reach them from all sides.

• Flowers will be ready for you to pick around three months from sowing or planting.

- Mulching with home-made compost or well-rotted manure once a year will help improve the structure of your soil and retain moisture, meaning less watering may be needed.

- Some staking may be necessary to support taller plants or encourage straighter stems. Ready-made supports are attractive but expensive, so have a think about reusing bamboo canes or hazel sticks. Some shorter plants may still flop over in wet or windy weather, so stretching netting with a wide-open mesh (such as pea netting) between some bamboo canes will provide the extra help they need.

- If space is limited, it's easy to add cut flowers into what you're growing already. Simply scatter large groups of annuals, bulbs or biennials among your existing plants. This is also a good way to provide plenty of flowers for picking without spoiling your existing display.

TOP TO BOTTOM Alliums; tulips and daffodils.

WHERE TO GROW

- Containers work just as well for growing most cut flowers, so don't hold back from growing them in this way. Shorter plants will work better than those with tall or floppy stems.

- Choose a sunny, open site that is reasonably sheltered and away from trees.

- Try and avoid a part of the garden that gets particularly frosty if you can.

What to grow

The cut flowers you grow will be determined by your space, situation and personal taste. There is a huge range to choose from, so why not pick a few from each category below to find your own winning combination.

ANNUALS

Annuals will be the mainstay of your cut flower patch. They're cheap and easy to grow, and if picked regularly will give you lots of flowers again and again.

For the best arrangements, don't forget about foliage. You might think you already have plenty in the rest of the garden, but if you add a few foliage filler plants you will be able to make a more balanced arrangement that doesn't look too formal.

Overleaf you'll find some suggestions of annuals to try. These can be grown in combination with those listed in earlier chapters for a long-lasting mix of flowers and foliage.

TOP TO BOTTOM Honeywort; scabious.

Dill Lovely, airy, acid-green flowers that give a light, sophisticated touch to arrangements.

Hare's ear (*Bupleurum rotundifolium*) Bright-green flowers with foliage that looks great alongside richer, bolder hues or soft whites.

Honeywort Grey-green leaves and bell-shaped flowers that go from deep blue to sumptuous purple.

Annual mallow (*Malope trifida*) The variety 'Vulcan' comes in eye-popping magenta with an unexpected lime-green centre. The silky petals seem to catch the light and will be a real talking point whether in the garden or in a vase.

Bunny tails This playful grass has beautifully soft flower heads that add lovely texture and movement.

Scabious Try 'Black Knight' for purple-black velvet pom-pom flowers on long wiry stems. In a sheltered spot it may even flower well into autumn and early winter.

Sweet peas Flowering early and abundantly, a few wigwams of these will pack a punch with scent and colour.

VASES, BOTTLES OR BOWLS?

It's worth building up a collection of vases to really make the most of your flowers. There's no point in going to all the trouble of growing and collecting them only to put them in any old container! Keep these simple options in your cupboard and you won't go wrong.

Vases

If you only have room for one, aim for a medium-sized, clear glass vase with a round body and a smaller neck. This will make arranging easier.

A simple, tall, clear glass vase is wonderful for long-stemmed flowers, such as cleomes or delphiniums. Just a few of these in a vase will make a real statement.

If you want something cheap and cheerful, scour charity shops, flea markets, online auction sites and car boot sales for small, coloured glass bottles or bud vases. If you want a display of little crocuses or grass flower heads on your desk, these will do the job beautifully.

Bottles

Sometimes simple is best. There may be times when you want to display something just by itself, and a slim glass bottle is ideal for this. This is a nice way to display alliums or the more elaborate tulip forms.

Bowls

Some flowers are best appreciated by floating them in bowls. Hellebores look wonderful displayed in this way, where you can really enjoy the scattering of delicate pink freckles across the petals. Choose a large shallow bowl and make sure the stems are cut very short.

Hellebores.

IDEAS FOR FOLIAGE

Glossy-leaved evergreens have their place but can give a dark and heavy feel if overused. Try these suggestions for a light and modern look.

- Schilling spurge (*Euphorbia schillingii*)
- Dark-leaved cow parsley (*Anthriscus sylvestris* 'Ravenswing')
- Golden marjoram (*Origanum vulgare* 'Aurea')
- Copper beech (*Fagus sylvatica f. purpurea*)
- Tawhiwhi (*Pittosporum tenuifolium*)
- Argyle apple (*Eucalyptus cinerea*)
- Laurustinus (*Viburnum tinus*)
- Japanese spiraea (*Spiraea japonica*) (shown below)

HALF HARDY ANNUALS

These plants can't tolerate frost but will make an excellent addition to your display. Start them off on your windowsill or in a propagator, following the steps in Chapter 1.

Get your plants used to cooler conditions by putting them outside during the day and bringing them in at night. If you have a cold frame, leave the lid off during the day.

Remove the very top of your plant using your forefinger and thumb, leaving a couple of buds or side shoots below (this is called 'pinching out'). Do this before you plant them outside, as this will encourage them to be bushier and produce more flowers. They're safe to be planted outside once all risk of frost has passed, usually late May or early June.

Purple vervain (*Verbena bonariensis*) Tall but with an airy structure that looks wonderful when left to self-seed throughout your beds and borders. Loved by bees and butterflies.

Snapdragon A long flowering period and a decent vase life too. Try it in coral pink, apricot, crimson red or white.

Rudbeckia The annual forms are smaller than the perennial varieties and will look good in containers too. Try 'Cherry Brandy' for a dark wine colour that will last for ages in a vase.

Spider flower (*Cleome hassleriana*) Tall and dramatic, just a single stem in a vase or bottle makes an impact. Grow from fresh seed for best results.

TOP TO BOTTOM
Purple vervain; snapdragon; rudbeckia; spider flower.

TIPS FOR A STUNNING (AND SIMPLE) ARRANGEMENT

Embrace asymmetry You can make your arrangement fun and less rigid by allowing branches and stems to go in different directions and by using odd numbers of your main flower.

Bring the garden indoors Let your flower heads and stems sit and fall as they would outdoors to make your arrangement look natural and flowing.

Give it the 3D effect Even if your display is against a window or wall, make it look interesting by avoiding the approach of having tall stems at the back and short ones at the front.

Contrasting colour Use a colour wheel to help you think about colours that contrast with each other (such as red and blue, orange and purple). Using contrasting colours makes your arrangement look fun and appealing. If you want lots of different colours, limit your choice of flowers.

BIENNIALS

These will form roots and leaves in their first year, then flower, set seed and die in the second. They are easy to grow from seed and most will keep producing flowers if picked regularly. Those listed below can be sown straight into the ground from May to July.

Sweet william These flowers make useful fillers, with the spiky buds creating an unusual texture in arrangements.

Foxglove The stately stems of foxgloves look striking in the garden as well as in a vase. Wild forms will happily self-seed throughout the garden, or you could try cultivars such as 'Sutton's Apricot' for a sophisticated splash of creamy peach.

Honesty Sturdy and tall, these create dreamy swathes of purple or white that will be the perfect base for late spring arrangements. The round silvery seedheads can be dried and look beautiful in a vase on their own. If you're after good seedheads and don't mind smaller flowers, you can grow these as an annual if sown early enough.

Sea holly Once cut this won't produce more flowers so be sure to grow plenty of it as its striking architectural qualities will make it a firm favourite. Use fresh or dried.

TOP TO BOTTOM
Sweet william; foxglove; honesty; sea holly.

90

PERENNIALS

For a dedicated cut flower patch, you won't need many perennials. Two or three of the following suggestions will bulk up your selection and provide a reliable base from which to experiment and have fun with your annuals.

Globe thistle These spiky, lollipop-shaped flowers add playful texture to an arrangement and also work really well when dried. Try 'Blue Globe' for large flower heads.

Helenium In a wide range of warm hues, these long-lasting daisy-like flowers add a real pop of colour. Use 'Sahin's Early Flowerer' for sunset oranges and yellows.

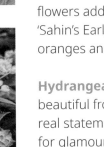

Hydrangea Even on their own, these beautiful frothy flower domes make a real statement. Try H. *paniculata* types for glamour, or the classic H. *microphylla* for long-lasting colour.

Rosemary As well as adding perfume to your arrangement, rosemary has charming flowers from deep to pale blue. This will add a touch of evergreen to winter arrangements.

TOP TO BOTTOM
Globe thistle; helenium; hydrangea; rosemary.

Giant oat grass The stunning flower heads of these grasses give height and a lovely airy feel.

Seasonal picks

Depending on what you already have in your outdoor space, it's possible that there will be something that you can pick and use fresh all year round. Don't forget about other features such as seedpods, colourful bare stems or the hips on roses – these can look really striking in combination with other fresh flowers or on their own.

SPRING
Lilac
Daffodil
Euphorbia
Hyacinth
Tulip
Peony
Magnolia
Crocus

SUMMER
Snapdragon
Poppy
Allium
Rose
Lily
Dill
Dianthus
Cosmos
Zinnia
Sunflower

AUTUMN
Dahlia
Helenium
Aster
Penstemon

WINTER
Cornus
Willow
Hellebore
Viburnum
Witch hazel

How to pick flowers

This is probably the most fun part – a chance to wander around and admire your hard work, surrounded by a riot of colour and texture that you've created. Follow these simple steps on how to pick your own cut flowers to help your beautiful blooms last longer in the vase.

Cut when it's cool Try to cut in the early morning or early evening. Plants are less likely to droop straight away from a loss of moisture at these times than if you cut in the middle of the day.

Take care of your tools Use sharp secateurs or florists' scissors, and make sure they're as sharp as possible to avoid damaging any of the stems.

FLORISTRY KIT

This is not an exhaustive list, but it will help get you started on creating those picture-worthy arrangements you've been dreaming about.

Flower scissors Should be light but sharp enough to cut through wire and stems.

Twine To secure bunches.

Floral tape To hold flower stems in place without damaging them.

Support wire To help strengthen stems and attach them to wreaths, or for securing other objects, such as bows and ribbon.

Foliage stripper Makes removing thorns and unnecessary foliage quick and easy.

Cut sensibly Try to pick from the back of a shrub or larger plant so you don't spoil the display. Take a few stems from several plants rather than all from one.

Keep your stems long A longer stem will give you more options when it comes to arranging and can always be trimmed if necessary.

Water As soon as your plant has been picked, put it in a bucket of water that's about one-third full. Some plants will never recover if they're not put in water straight away. Doing this is one of the best ways to ensure a longer vase life.

Separate sizes Keep short and tall plants in different containers to avoid crushing and damaging your precious flowers.

Strip Remove the bottom leaves and any unnecessary side shoots as you go. This will save you a job later and help reduce the surface area from which the plant will be losing moisture as soon as it's picked.

Be adventurous Have fun! Don't just go for the obvious and, most importantly, pick what you love. Tasteful pastels have their place but don't forget about richer, bolder colours and shapes too.

Be your own florist

You don't need expensive floral foam to have a go at these simple arrangements, just a bit of time and imagination will do.

Hand-tied bouquet

For the perfect gift, try a simple hand-tied bunch of your own home-grown flowers. Use bright, cheerful blooms or keep the colour palette simple for a more sophisticated look.

1   Lay out your flowers and foliage into separate piles.

2   In one hand, build up your first layer using the main foliage you want to try, such as euphorbia or bupleurum. Try to make the top of the arrangement into a nice rounded dome shape.

3   Use one hand to hold your bunch and the other to add your stems. This will make it easier for you to check the shape as you go. Push the stems in at a slight angle and then pull them through from the bottom – this will avoid damaging any flower heads.

4 When adding your flowers, odd
numbers often look more pleasing.

5 Once you're happy with your
arrangement, add string or ribbon to
tie the stems together securely. Then
just cut off the ends of the stems to
the same length.

Dried flowers

Dried flowers look good on their own, last for ages and are a fun way to create interesting shapes and textures.

Lots of plants are great for dried arrangements, including eryngium, lavender, limonium, golden oats (*Stipa gigantea*) or the beautifully papery everlasting flower.

1   Once cut, combine your plants into small bunches and tie with string. Hang upside down somewhere cool and dry for at least a couple of weeks.

2   Lay out the dried flowers and foliage in separate piles.

3   Start arranging your foliage first, stem by stem, then add your flowers. A narrow-necked vase can help keep the stems in place.

4   Experiment with different heights and don't be afraid of asymmetry. Trim the stems as you go to get the variation in height you want.

5   Add your flowers all the way round, not just at the front, to keep the arrangement modern and interesting from all angles.

Sophisticated stems

For a simple and elegant winter or early spring display, all you need is a large vase and an odd number of interesting stems. Try hazel (with catkins for extra drama), pussy willow or cornus, as well as stems with emerging spring leaves or blossom, such as cherry, amelanchier or viburnum. Don't be afraid to go big – a large vase or container and beautifully arching stems adds real drama.

1   Add pebbles or glass marbles to the bottom of your vase to help stabilise your branches if desired.

2   Fill your vase one-third full of water and remove any side branches that might sit in the water or create an awkward shape.

3   Cut a shallow slit across the bottom of the stems to aid water uptake.

4   Add your branches to the vase, arranging them at alternate angles.

Foraging

Foraging is a great way to spend time in nature, relieve stress and connect with the world around you. You can find and gather objects, such as pine cones, old seedheads or a few pieces of foliage to bring some seasonal finishing touches to your arrangements, all for free. Foraging responsibly like this will help you create something unique to you, without breaking the bank or damaging the natural environment. Pieces to look out for could include:

- The glossy leaves and flower buds of ivy or the fluffy seedheads of *Clematis vitalba* (also known as old man's beard) add a three-dimensional touch to an arrangement.

- Holly berries and rosehips make eye-catching additions to wreaths, and can be kept somewhere cool and dry for use later. Be sure to leave plenty for wildlife.

- Feathers, twigs coated in beautiful lichen, or dried-out seedheads can make striking objects for display. Use on their own in glass jars or bottles, or incorporate into a flower arrangement.

- Fallen autumn leaves can be collected, pressed between the pages of a book to dry, then used to decorate a seasonal wreath.

- Washed-up seashells (provided there's nothing living inside them) are another way to add a decorative layer in vases to support stems.

FORAGED CHRISTMAS WREATH

Making a wreath with foraged material will mean you've created something fresh, unique and sustainable.

You will need
- Bendy stems from hazel or willow (soaking willow in cold water in the bath or kitchen sink for 24 hours makes it more pliable)
- Foraged material (such as ivy, yew, holly, pine cones, rosehips)
- Garden string; brown jute string will blend in more easily
- 2 hours

1   To make it easier to create a circle for your wreath, you can bend the stems around a reusable metal wreath frame or go freehand by twisting two or three of the stems together if you prefer a more rustic look.

2   Tie a loop of string at the top of your wreath ready for hanging.

3   Add your foraged foliage first, starting with larger-leaved items like holly.

4   To attach pine cones, wrap a length of string around the middle of each one and tie a knot. Your string should be long enough so that there are two free ends either side of each pine cone, which you can then use to tie them to your wreath.

5   Add the finishing touches with smaller-leaved foliage and more delicate items such as berries.

THE FORAGER'S CODE

- Don't take anything that is rare or endangered. Check the Woodland Trust's website for advice.

- Never dig up plants and remove them.

- Avoid taking too much from one area – leave enough for others, as well as bees and other insects.

- Get the landowner's permission to forage on private land.

5. Indoor Plants

There's no doubt that being around greenery can reduce our stress levels and improve our focus. Just spending a few minutes tending plants can help redirect anxiety and channel our energy into something positive and productive.

As well as making us feel better, plants help our indoor areas look better, transforming a sterile space into something warm and inviting. With houseplants, the world really is your oyster. Whether it's desert succulents or leafy tropical palms, there is a houseplant (or several) to suit you.

How to choose a houseplant

Right plant, right room Think about the conditions you have to offer in different rooms. What are the light levels like? Are there any draughts? Is it cool or warm? Many houseplants prefer a bright spot, but one where sunlight does not shine directly on the leaves, which can cause scorching. Some will prefer a darker area, so assess your conditions and pick accordingly.

Aftercare How much time do you have to spend watering and are you likely to remember? If you're away a lot, you may need plants that are more drought-tolerant and won't shrivel up sadly after a few days.

Perfect pot It's a good idea to make sure your houseplant can drain away any excess moisture. Try to have two containers – one that your plant is potted up in that has drainage holes in the bottom, and a more decorative container for it to sit in. You can always place a shallow dish inside your decorative pot for any excess water to collect if needed.

DOS AND DON'TS FOR THRIVING HOUSEPLANTS

Do keep your plant in one place if it's happy. Sudden changes in temperature and humidity caused by moving plants around too often or too quickly can cause them to lose vigour.

Do dust your plants from time to time to make sure the leaves are able to make the most of the light and keep on photosynthesising.

Do feed occasionally. You can buy houseplant food online or from garden centres. This is a good idea if you're not able to keep re-potting your plants into fresh compost.

Do rotate plants if you can so they grow evenly and don't lean too much in one direction to reach the light.

Don't water too often. Once a week in summer and less often in winter is a good general rule but try to look carefully to see what your plant needs, rather than sticking rigidly to a schedule. If in doubt, check the top few centimetres of compost – if it's dry, then water.

Don't put plants near a radiator or anywhere too draughty as big fluctuations in temperature can put them under a lot of stress.

Style tips

Follow these simple suggestions to style your houseplants like a pro.

Look for colour and texture When selecting artwork for your wall, you wouldn't choose pictures that were all identical, and the same goes for houseplants. Think about plants with colours and patterns, such as the prayer plant (*Maranta leuconeura*), or interesting leaf shapes like the ZZ plant (*Zamioculcas zamiifolia*).

Play with scale Don't be afraid to mix up large and small plants. Smaller specimens will look brilliant on a bookshelf or side table, while a palm or yucca in a large pot on the floor will add interest to an awkward corner. Placing plants at different heights will make the most of features, such as the trailing stems on either an ivy (*Hedera helix*) or string of pearls (*Senecio rowleyanus*).

Mix it up Incorporate houseplants into your existing home accessories in bookcases or on shelves. Plants look wonderful alongside books, vases and sculptures.

Complement your decor If your space is minimal and de-cluttered, then containers with clean lines in neutral tones will suit you best. If pattern and colour is more your thing, then scour the internet and vintage markets for pots with unique shapes and colour combinations.

Bold and beautiful Place plants in front of bold wallpaper designs to create a pleasing contrast. Palms work particularly well like this as you can catch glimpses of the bright design through the fronds.

Look up To liven up your displays and add a touch of green anywhere, think about going vertical. Try a floating shelf suspended from the ceiling, or pots hanging from hooks and racks, even your shower curtain rail. A wall-mounted shelf above the bed is an inexpensive and easy way to add plants to a small space.

Plant stands If you want to devote a specific corner of your room to plants, then a plant stand is invaluable. In a range of materials, styles and colours to suit your decor, this is a brilliant option for renters – no need to drill holes in the walls and ceiling, and you can easily take your plant stand with you.

Fuss-free Want to avoid the mess and fuss of compost and pots? Try air plants. Also known as *Tillandsia*, these plants are easy to care for and can be tied onto a piece of bark in the bathroom, put into air plant holders to hang from the ceiling or placed on a coffee table in the living room.

SUSTAINABLE HOUSEPLANTS

Top tips for an eco-friendly approach to building your collection of indoor plants.

- Use peat-free compost when potting up your plants.

- Propagate your own plants from division or grow from seed.

- Buy second-hand pots and shelving units to create beautiful displays.

- Cut down on plastic. Reuse existing plastic pots and support growers who avoid plastic packaging.

- Join a plant society. It's a great way to build up knowledge about plants you love, and gain access to seeds and plants that have not been collected from the wild.

HOW TO WATER SUCCULENTS

Succulents such as aloes and the jade plant can be susceptible to rotting if they are watered too often. This is especially true in winter when colder temperatures combined with soggy compost can be disastrous.

An easy way to water succulents is to place the pot they're planted in into a bucket or sink about one-third filled with water. By watering from the bottom, they're able to take up as much liquid as they need and it's much easier to avoid overwatering them.

If your pot doesn't have drainage holes, make sure your succulent is in a gritty compost mix to allow water to evaporate quickly. Use a measuring jug or cup to help you pour in a small amount of water at a time. This will help you see the optimum amount for your specific container. Using a tap for watering can cause you to flood the plant with too much water.

Only water again when the compost is completely dry.

KOKODAMA

A Japanese version of a hanging basket, this is simple to make and can be hung indoors or out. Suitable plants for outdoors use include ivy (as described here), cyclamen or violas. Indoor kokodamas could use orchids (shown opposite), asparagus fern or string of pearls.

You will need
- Multipurpose peat-free compost
- Sharp sand
- 1 small ivy plant
- Garden twine
- Scissors
- Sustainable sheet moss (can be sourced online)
- 1–2 hours

1   First make your compost mix. Add 2 parts sharp sand to 4 parts multipurpose compost as this will help improve the drainage. Add water as you go until the mixture resembles a wet cake mix.

2 Remove any old soil from the roots of your ivy.

3 Pack the fresh compost mix around the ivy roots. Make sure there are no gaps. Try to make a ball shape around the roots with the wet compost.

4 Place a sheet of moss on a table and put your ivy in the centre. Wrap the moss around the compost (you might need an extra pair of hands

for this). Make sure all compost is covered by the moss.

5 Wind twine around the moss ball until it's securely held in place. Leave a length of sting long enough to hang it up with and cut off any excess.

6 Keep your kokodama out of direct sunlight and dip it into a bucket of water regularly. Misting with water will also help keep it moist.

Plants for the living room

The focal point of your home can be made to feel more welcoming with the inclusion of just a few well-chosen houseplants. A bright spot near a window will suit many different varieties, but don't worry if light is limited as there are still plenty of great options to choose from.

Ivy (*Hedera helix*)
If you are looking for a plant that is easy-going, then why not try a pot of ivy on a windowsill or side table where you can appreciate its trailing stems. Ivy adds a traditional, romantic touch to a room and is a good 'starter' plant for houseplant novices.

Devil's ivy (*Epipremnum aureum*)

This is probably one of the most undemanding houseplants. Native to French Polynesia in the South Pacific, this beautiful vine with glossy arrowhead-shaped leaves is happy in bright or low light, and can even survive just in a vase of water. Variegated varieties are attractive but will need more light to keep the colour in their leaves.

Fiddle-leaf fig (*Ficus lyrata*)

Many varieties of fig make excellent houseplants, but this specimen is particularly striking. Large violin-shaped leaves make a real statement and look great by patio doors or a large window. It's a fast-grower, and while it prefers the steamy conditions of tropical Africa, it will tolerate a typical living room in the UK.

Peace lily (*Spathiphyllum spp.*)

Peace lilies give a lush, tropical feel to a room and don't require a lot of space. They will flower more often in a brighter spot but are tolerant of low light levels too. Check once a week for watering and if the top of the compost feels moist then leave it alone. Peace lilies do not appreciate being overwatered so be sure to only give them a drink when they really need it.

ZZ plant (*Zamioculcas zamiifolia*)

If you have a dark corner that's in need of something interesting, then try the ZZ plant. Perfect for beginners, it is extremely hardy and will take neglect in its stride. Water about once a week but less often if light levels are low. Don't let it be ingested by children or pets: as with most house plants, the leaves are toxic.

Dragon tree (*Dracaena marginata*)

Narrow strap-like leaves create an architectural focal point with this undemanding plant from Madagascar. It likes the compost to be moist but not too wet – if yellow or droopy leaves appear, you may have overdone it. It will be perfectly happy at average room temperature, but prefers a bright spot.

Polka dot begonia (*Begonia maculata*)

If you would like to add a tropical feel to your living room, then this striking plant from the lush forests of Brazil might be just the thing. If you can offer reasonable light levels and a warm room, then it's a good one to try. This plant has a lot going for it looks-wise: silvery spotted leaves with deep red undersides; tall cane-like stems; and clusters of white, pink or red flowers. It really hates soggy soil so only water once the top few centimetres of compost have dried out.

MARIMO MOSS BALLS

For a houseplant that needs minimal care and looks good all the time, try Marimo. Although commonly called moss balls, these are actually an unusual form of velvety green spherical algae.

- Easily sourced from aquarium shops or online, they are simple to take care of – just add water.

- Try adding pebbles or pieces of driftwood to the jar they are kept in to create a soothing underwater display.

- Keep them out of direct light or they'll turn brown.

- Change the water they're living in every couple of weeks (tap water is fine).

- To keep them round and stop them going flat, agitate the water every so often. This will ensure they rest on a slightly different side than previously.

Plants for the bathroom

Bathrooms are a happy place for lots of houseplants. Many varieties hail from tropical climates, so the steamy, humid atmosphere in a bathroom will help your plants to thrive. If you don't have a window you'll need to get creative, but you can still enjoy a rainforest feel. Choose plants that prefer low light levels, move them occasionally to increased light when you can, and consider investing in a grow light to keep them happy and healthy.

Snake plant (*Sansevieria trifasciata*)
This tropical plant from West Africa enjoys bright light but will also cope well with lower light levels. It enjoys high humidity but avoid overwatering in the winter months as this will be fatal. Its upright stems look striking in a simple cylindrical or straight-sided pot for a clean, minimal look.

Spider plant (*Chlorophytum comosum*)
An adaptable and easy houseplant, this will enjoy the conditions offered by a bathroom. Place on a high windowsill where its baby plantlets can hang down easily. It will tolerate shadier spots but will grow less quickly. It's also easily divided as it grows so you can create more plants for other parts of your home.

Spider plant.

Boston fern (*Nephrolepis exaltata*)

This beautiful evergreen fern loves warmth and humidity and prefers low light levels, so it is perfect for the bathroom. Ferns generally prefer moist conditions so make sure its compost doesn't dry out. This plant can get quite big, so indulge in a large pot that complements your decor and enjoy the texture of its fronds.

Inch plant (*Tradescantia zebrina*)

With green, purple, and silver foliage, the trailing stems of the inch plant look striking cascading from a shelf or windowsill. If you have a tendency to neglect your plants, then this one will be very forgiving.

Bromeliad (*Guzmania spp.*)

Many bromeliads hail from the warm climates of the tropical Americas, so if you have a bright spot in your bathroom that needs an extra pop of colour, try one of these. In the spring and summer months they produce a colourful arrangement of modified leaves (called bracts) on a tall stem. This can make them top heavy, so provide a sturdy container. When this central stem dies back, cut it down close to the compost and allow the new baby bromeliads to grow.

TOP TO BOTTOM
Boston fern; inch plant; bromeliad.

Plants for the bedroom

Having some plants in this part of your home can reduce your stress levels, boost your mood in the winter months and help improve sleep by purifying the air you breathe. A calm and serene atmosphere can be created with the addition of just a few pots here and there. If space is at a premium, try hanging plants. A clothing rack with plants suspended from it can be a useful room divider as well as a fun way to incorporate greenery.

Areca palm (*Dypsis lutescens*)
With a smooth trunk and narrow, elegant fronds, these palms certainly have presence. A bright room and a large container are a must, as is well-drained compost. Misting the leaves occasionally will help raise the humidity which the plant will definitely enjoy.

Chinese evergreen (*Aglaonema commutatum*)

The attractively speckled leaves of this plant really stand out when combined with the glossy leaves of devil's ivy or the peace lily. It is an easy one to start out with and suitable for low light levels.

Lady palm (*Rhapis excelsa*)

This slow-growing palm is unfussy and definitely creates a feel of lush greenery. It is an excellent plant for purifying the air and is suitable for bedrooms with low light levels. If you want well-behaved and easy, this is the perfect palm for you.

Chinese money plant
(*Pilea peperomioides*)

With flat coin-shaped leaves, almost like a lily pad, this plant is easy to care for and will produce lots of baby plants for you to give away as gifts or use to bulk up your collection. They don't mind a small amount of direct light and will grow best in warm conditions. If the leaves start to curl or bend, this could be due to insufficient light and may need moving to a brighter spot. Water thoroughly and then leave alone to almost dry out before watering again.

KEEPING PLANTS ALIVE IN WINTER

As temperatures drop outside and the heating goes on, this can create a new set of challenges for your houseplants. Here's how to keep them healthy during the colder months.

Don't overwater Although the air will be drier thanks to the heating being on, lower light levels will mean plant growth slows down. The surface of the compost may dry out quickly so check to see what's going on deeper down, about 2.5cm (1in) or so. If you can see darker soil then there's still some moisture there.

Raise humidity Group your plants together if you can. Moisture is released through pores, the majority of which are on the undersides of the leaves. Placing your plants together means they can share some of that released moisture. Misting helps but needs to be done regularly, so you may be better off with trays of water. Add pebbles to the trays and sit your pots on top.

Keep it bright Some plants may need to be moved to take advantage of brighter light levels in a different part of the house. Be mindful though of sudden changes in temperature or potential draughts – it might be worth acclimatising them gradually to a new spot.

Terrariums

From the Latin for 'enclosed earth', terrariums are a perfect way to create your own slice of horticultural heaven. With the right container and plants, you can create an enclosed little world that resembles a mini tropical jungle or desert landscape.

Go for clear glass in simple shapes such as spheres or cubes. If using cacti and succulents, you'll need a more open container like a large fishbowl to create a drier environment. For tropical plants, you'll need to make sure the opening at the top of your container is narrow enough to trap humidity and warmth, or choose one that comes with a lid.

Making sure your container is large enough for soil and air movement is also important for a successful terrarium and will give your plants room to grow. If you want to keep it miniature, try slow-growing aquatic plants rather than ferns or palms.

A POTTED HISTORY

The first terrarium was discovered by accident by Dr Nathaniel Bagshaw Ward in the 19th century. He was a keen observer of the natural world, and one day collected a moth cocoon, some fern leaves and soil. After sealing it all up in a glass bottle, it was left for three years. Eventually he noticed that the fern was starting to sprout and grow, thriving in its little tropical microclimate within the glass bottle.

This inspired him to create a glass case to help transport live plants from across the world. A friend of his successfully used these cases on a plant-collecting expedition between England and Australia, and found that 95 per cent of the specimens survived the journey. This type of case became known as a 'Wardian' case and went on to transform the world of botanical exploration.

HOW TO MAKE A TERRARIUM

You will need
- Glass container
- Small pebbles or stones
- Activated charcoal (available online; a sprinkle of this helps prevent the build-up of bacteria)
- Peat-free potting compost
- Small, slow-growing plants (tillandsia, inch plant or fittonia are ideal)
- Sustainably sourced moss (optional)
- 30 minutes–1 hour

1   Make sure your container is clean and dry. At the bottom of it add a 2–3cm (approx. 1in) layer of pebbles or stones to aid drainage.

2   Scatter the charcoal over the stones.

3   Add a layer of potting compost. This needs to be deep enough for your chosen plants to sit in comfortably.

4   Start with your largest plant first and make a hole in the compost big enough for it to sit in. Backfill and cover the roots.

5   Add your remaining plants. Make sure they aren't pressed against the glass and have enough room to grow a little.

6   You can add some sustainably sourced moss to create a soft effect and to cover up the soil if you wish.

7   Keep out of direct light and aim to mist the plants with water every couple of weeks or when the compost is looking dry. If you are using cacti and succulents instead, these prefer drier air so avoid misting them as they may start to rot.

6. Grow Your Own

If you want fresh fruit, veg and herbs at your fingertips then it's time to start growing your own. Not only is nurturing fruit and veg hugely rewarding, but it can also save you money. It's easier than you may think to grow food, no matter how much – or how little – space you have, and you won't have to worry about chemicals and food miles. Whether you have a windowsill or a dedicated veg garden, here's what to grow for perfectly delicious produce all year round.

Herbs

Herbs are brilliant for adding flavour to a huge range of dishes. All of the following can easily be grown in raised beds, containers on a balcony or in pots on a windowsill, although some may prefer a brighter spot than others. The more you pick, the bushier your plant will get, so don't hold back on adding fresh flavours to your salads and stir-fries on a regular basis.

FOR A SUNNY SPOT

Thyme To give extra depth to your Sunday roast you can't beat fresh thyme. Finely chopped over roast potatoes, this aromatic shrub is hardy and has flowers that bees love too. Trim after flowering to keep it compact.

Basil This plant comes in many forms so why not experiment with growing purple, cinnamon or Thai basil? Basil likes warm, moist conditions in a bright spot. Pinch out the tips regularly to keep it producing fresh leaves.

Potted basil.

PRESERVING

If you have a glut of herbs and are not sure what to do with them, try these simple suggestions for preserving your produce.

Drying Some herbs, such as thyme and rosemary, retain their flavour when dried. Tie stems into bunches and hang somewhere cool and dry.

Steeping Infuse a good-quality olive oil with fresh basil leaves.

Freezing Some herbs disintegrate after being frozen, but mint and chives freeze well. Snip chives into sections, put into ice-cube trays and freeze without water. Freeze mint leaves in ice-cube trays with water – these are delicious in cool drinks.

Herb butter Chop your fresh herb of choice and mix into softened butter with a pinch of sea salt.

Oregano Trailing varieties look good in window boxes or around the edges of larger containers. Strip the leaves from the stem to add punchy flavour to rich tomato-based sauces or to make a soothing tea.

Lemon verbena Aromatic and fresh, the leaves of lemon verbena give a subtle citrus flavour to teas and cakes. It may need some protection from hard frosts.

Lemon verbena.

COMPANION PLANTING

Known as companion planting, growing herbs and flowering plants alongside fruit and veg can help to deter pests, attract pollinators and improve the flavour of your crop. Aromatic herbs are particularly good at deterring aphids, while nasturtium can act as a 'decoy' plant, attracting caterpillars who will feast on it instead of your precious veggies. Here's what to grow together for a beautiful and healthy plot.

Chamomile The strong scent helps deter various brassica pests including cabbage butterflies and can work well planted alongside fruit trees to prevent fungal infections.

Summer savory Helps to ward off blackfly, a common pest with broad beans. It is said to help improve the flavour of onions and shallots.

Rosemary Another great companion plant to go alongside brassicas and help discourage cabbage moth.

Curry plant This strongly scented herb can deter aphids and flea beetles.

Borage Bees and butterflies are drawn to the blue flowers, ensuring your crops will be pollinated. It's also said to improve the flavour of strawberries.

Pot marigold Attracts beneficial insects such as hoverflies which will feast on aphids, as well as discouraging whitefly and aphids.

FOR A SHADY SPOT

Parsley Perfectly happy in pots but keep well-watered in dry spells to prevent the leaves turning yellow. Use as a garnish or to flavour fish and chicken dishes.

Chives The cheerful pom-pom shaped flowers of chives are as edible as the leaves and give fresh colour to your salads and soups. To harvest, simply snip away with your scissors – it couldn't be easier.

Coriander This herb will thrive in partial shade and is easy to grow from seed. You can eat the leaves, stems and seeds, which can be used as a garnish or to add rich flavour to soups, meatballs and rice dishes.

Mint The possibilities are many for this lovely herb, so for something a little different try lemon or chocolate mint as well as the usual peppermint and spearmint. Mint is quite happy in a pot too.

TOP TO BOTTOM Coriander; chives; mint.

Salad leaves

There is a whole host of delicious and wonderfully flavoured leaves you can grow to liven up your salads. These tasty plants are compact, versatile and can be grown on your balcony, in a veg plot or on a windowsill.

Mustard Warm and peppery flavours can be found in this wonderful addition to any salad. Leaves become a little fiery with age, so it's best to pick young ones. Try 'Red Giant' with its attractive burgundy leaves. It looks lovely in pots or as edging around a raised bed.

Rocket Don't forget about eating the flowers of this salad staple. Although known for its peppery taste, combine with radicchio to bring out its sweeter side. A great 'cut and come again' crop, regular harvesting will reward you with fresh new leaves for weeks.

Tatsoi Quick and easy to grow from seed, this has a subtle flavour similar to spinach. It prefers cooler growing conditions so keep growing and harvesting until May, then resume in September.

Mizuna Similar to rocket in appearance and with a subtle warm flavour. The deeply cut leaves create a lovely change in texture when grown with other salad crops.

Lambs' lettuce Used in the same way as spinach but with a tangier flavour. It forms a small rosette of spoon-shaped leaves and should be harvested whole for best results. A good choice for autumn sowing as it's remarkably cold tolerant.

Shungiku Also known as chrysanthemum greens or chop suey greens, this is best used when the leaves and stems are young and tender for an aromatic and mildly bitter hit of flavour. The petals from the flowers are also edible and will beautify your salad in moments.

BEST MICROGREENS TO GROW

Coriander
Basil
Spinach
Beetroot
Mizuna
Fennel

How to grow

1 Fill your chosen container with peat-free multipurpose compost (or seed compost if you have it) and firm gently.

2 Moisten the compost by watering overhead using a watering can with a fine rose, or if using pots, place them in a large tub of water until the top of the compost starts to darken (you can always use the kitchen sink for this).

3 Sow the seeds and cover them lightly with sifted compost.

4 Place somewhere bright and keep moist. They'll be ready to harvest a week or two after sowing.

INDOOR SALADS

Microgreens are an easy way to obtain all the flavour and nutritional benefits of a bigger plant but in miniature form. They are the seedlings of leafy veg or herbs that would normally be grown to maturity before harvesting.

Whatever container you have available will work, whether it's a yoghurt pot, butter tub or a plastic bottle cut lengthways. You can grow microgreens all year round as long as you have somewhere bright to put them.

Edible flowers

It's not just leafy greens that are edible, many flowers are too. They're the perfect way to decorate all manner of dishes for a pop of unexpected colour. Just make sure any flowers you use haven't been sprayed with pesticides and are picked as fresh as possible.

CAKES AND BAKES

What to use
Violas and pansies, rose petals, lavender buds.

How to use
• Crystallise violas and pansies to add a romantic touch to cakes that taste as sweet as they look (see page 138).

• Make lavender sugar by adding buds to granulated white sugar and leave for a week to allow the natural oils to infuse. Then use in place of regular sugar in your favourite biscuit and cake recipes.

• Stir in dried rose petals to the batter of your brownie mix.

SUGAR FLOWERS

It's easier than you may think to make your own crystallised flower cake decorations with these simple steps.

You will need
- Fresh flowers (try violas, pansies, rose petals, borage, primroses or blossom from apple or cherry)
- 1 egg white, lightly beaten
- Caster sugar
- Artist's paintbrush or teaspoon
- Drying rack or baking tray lined with parchment paper
- 1–2 hours

1 Make sure your chosen flowers are fresh and completely dry.

2 Dip the paintbrush, or teaspoon, into the egg white and lightly cover the front and back of the first flower.

3 Dip the flower into the caster sugar and gently tap off the excess.

4 Place on a drying rack or baking tray lined with parchment paper.

5 Repeat for the other flowers.

6 Leave to dry somewhere warm for 24 hours. Can be used straight away or stored in an airtight jar for several months.

SUMMER SALADS

What to use
Nasturtiums, pot marigold, chives, borage.

How to use
- Add nasturtium flowers whole to a mixed-leaf salad for a peppery hit, or deep-fry in a tempura batter.

- Sprinkle pot marigold petals over a salad, using a mix of orange, yellow and apricot shades to really make an impression.

- Chive flowers can be eaten whole or broken up into smaller segments for a subtle, fresh onion flavour.

- For a mild cucumber-like taste, add the flowers from borage. These are perfect for salads or adding to cold drinks.

ROASTS, SOUPS AND SAUCES

What to use
Fennel, dill, basil.

How to use
- For a fresh aniseed flavour that works well with meat and fish dishes, use fresh fennel flowers. Chop and rub into chicken before roasting, or steam with fresh veg.

- Chop fresh dill flowers and stir into soups, or mix with olive oil and salt and add to potatoes before roasting.

- Basil flowers can be used as well as the leaves for making pesto, or chop them finely and add to a tomato-based sauce with lemon juice and black pepper.

Easy veg

Growing your own veg is a lot of fun and a great way to get into gardening. You don't need a vast kitchen garden either; a surprising number of plants will be quite happy in a container, provided you can feed, water and harvest at regular intervals.

One thing to remember is to grow what you like to eat. There's no point having a pile of courgettes to get through if you can't stand them. You'll be much more motivated to spend the time looking after your veggies if you can have all the fun of cooking and eating them too.

Harvesting garlic.

NO ROOM TO ROTATE

Rotating your veg (growing it in a different spot each year) is a useful way to avoid a build-up of pests and diseases in the soil that can devastate a crop. It's useful if growing veg in large quantities but may not be particularly practical (or necessary) if you're only growing a few of something each year. With that in mind, here's how to keep your plants healthy year on year if space is at a premium.

- Remove any debris as soon as possible. Leaving old leaves lying around can give somewhere for pests to hide and encourage the spread of fungal diseases.

- Replenish the soil with organic matter. As this breaks down over time it will help improve the structure of your soil, allowing plants to access the nutrients they need more easily.

- When watering, aim to water the soil around your plants, rather than the foliage. This will help keep fungal problems to a minimum.

- Grow resistant varieties. Lots of modern veg varieties have been bred to resist various pests or diseases, so aim to grow these if you can.

- If in doubt about a pest or disease problem relating to a particular crop, avoid growing that specific vegetable for a year or two and then try again. This will give you the chance to try something new instead.

WINDOW BOXES

Chillies You'll need to wait for warmer weather before planting these outside, but once you do, you'll soon be rewarded with a good crop of deliciously fiery chillies. Harvest when green, or red for a fruitier flavour.

Garlic One of the easiest crops to grow. Split the bulb into individual cloves and plant each clove into peat-free multipurpose compost so the top is just covered. Different varieties are suitable for either autumn or spring planting, and you may need to water in dry spells. It is ready for harvesting once the leaves turn yellow.

Radishes Simply sow and go. Make a drill the length of your window box 1cm (½in) deep and water with a watering can and rose. Sprinkle the seeds thinly and cover them with compost. They'll be ready for harvesting within a few weeks.

Kohl rabi Globe-shaped, crisp and delicious, try a purple variety to add interesting colour to your stir-fries and slaw recipes. Harvest when golf-ball-sized for extra tenderness, but no bigger than a tennis ball or they start to get tough.

CONTAINERS

Bell peppers Grow in individual pots if space allows, or combine two or three plants in a larger container. Feed regularly once flowers appear to encourage the peppers to form. Tomato feed is cheap, easy to get hold of and perfect for the job.

Tomatoes Stick to smaller-fruited cherry varieties if planted in a shadier spot – these will need less sun to ripen. 'Tumbling Tom' is a hassle-free variety that doesn't need supports to grow up or the side shoots pinching out.

French beans (dwarf) In a large enough container you could combine two or three plants and choose from green, purple or spotted varieties. They may need some extra protection from slugs, but if harvested regularly, will keep on cropping.

Mangetout Add some bamboo canes around the sides of your container and tie in your young mangetout plants to encourage them to grow up the supports. 'Oregon Sugar Pod' is a superbly sweet and prolific variety that is delicious raw or cooked.

RAISED BEDS

Kale This works well in pots too, but if you have even just one or two raised beds this is well worth growing. A spring or summer sowing will keep you going with a steady crop if you harvest from the outer leaves inwards. It's even tough enough to withstand frosts.

Courgette In a small space, one or two plants are likely to be enough to keep you supplied with fresh courgettes. If space really is at a premium, try 'One Ball'; with small, rounded fruits that are just as tasty and versatile as the regular varieties.

Swiss chard This earthy flavoured leafy crop comes in a stunning array of colours, from deep scarlet to warm mustard yellow. Harvest from the outer leaves first and cook like spinach.

Onions An easy way to grow these is from 'sets', which are essentially baby onions you can pop directly into the ground. Leave just the tip showing when you plant them and cover them with netting so birds don't pull them out. You can remove this once leaves start to appear. Water in dry spells. They can be harvested fresh at any time if you're going to use them straight away, but if you want to store them wait until they're fully developed – this is when the leaves start to die back in late summer.

A SQUARE METRE VEG PLOT

- It's surprising what you can grow in just 1 sq. m (11 sq. ft). This is a method that is particularly suited to smaller plants and is a great way to have a go at veg growing within a manageable space.

- You can either have a 1 sq. m plot in the ground, or create a raised bed, ideally at least 30cm (12in) deep. If sitting your raised bed on a grass or soil base, line the bottom with cardboard and fill the bed with a mix of top soil, or a peat-free soil-based compost, such as John Innes No. 3, with some horticultural grit added. The layer of cardboard beneath will act as a weed suppresser but still allow veg roots to reach the soil beneath as it slowly decomposes.

- Divide the bed into 30cm (12in) squares. You can use string for this or buy a ready-made kit. Plant each square with either one large plant (e.g. tomato) or up to 16 smaller plants (e.g. radishes).

- These beds are relatively easy to maintain but can dry out quickly in warm weather so keep well-watered. Remove any weeds as soon as possible so they don't disturb the roots of your crop when you harvest.

- Suitable for: radishes, lettuce, herbs, bush tomatoes, turnips, swede, kohl rabi, carrots, parsnips, chilli pepper, kale, French beans (dwarf).

Unfussy fruit

When looking at growing fruit it's easy to be daunted by the many and varied pruning and training requirements, but it doesn't have to be complicated. Here are some suggestions for easy-to-maintain fruit for a delicious crop year after year.

Rhubarb This will need a decent amount of space, or a very large container, but is about as low-maintenance as it's possible to be. Once established, rhubarb can resent being moved, so choose your spot carefully, ideally one with plenty of sun. Harvest the stems from May to June, mulch the plant each year with a thick layer of compost or well-rotted manure, and enjoy the results in a good crumble!

Autumn-fruiting raspberries These are slightly easier to look after than summer-fruiting raspberries, and you can grow them in a large container. Once they've finished fruiting, simply cut all the canes down at once and mulch with manure or compost.

TOP TO BOTTOM Rhubarb; raspberries.

Strawberries Ideal in containers, window boxes and hanging baskets, or you can devote a whole bed to them if you prefer. Strawberries like full sun but will cope with partial shade. Water well in dry spells but try to avoid wetting the foliage or fruit as this can lead to fungal problems. You can mulch them with straw if you wish to help keep the fruit clean, but this isn't essential.

Goji berries Rich in antioxidants and vitamin C, you can eat these fresh or dried, pop them into drinks, enjoy them with your cereal or add to rice dishes. They will need full sun but are generally unfussy about soil type, and will be happy in a container as long as you feed and water regularly. The plant can take a while to get established so give it two or three years for fruit to appear.

Blackcurrants Generally quite a large shrub but smaller varieties (such as 'Ben Sarek') are available, which will suit a smaller space or a container. Blackcurrants need minimal pruning in winter. Simply remove some of the oldest stems at ground level to keep an open shape for plenty of air flow and fewer issues with fungal diseases.

TOP TO BOTTOM Strawberries; goji berries; blackcurrants.

7. Greener Gardening

However large or small your outdoor space, you have the potential to create a valuable ecosystem, and it's much easier than you may think. Creating wildlife-friendly areas means taking a step back and being a bit more relaxed. Don't be in a rush to cut back during autumn and winter as the seedheads from your flowering plants can be a valuable food source for birds, and the stems give insects somewhere to hide. If you have a lawn, consider leaving part of it to grow longer or turn some of it into a meadow. Think about constructing homes for insects to overwinter in, or sheltering spots for hedgehogs. Instead of reaching for the chemicals at the first sign of a pest invasion, accept that a certain amount of imperfection is not only inevitable but necessary to keep everything in balance. After all, if you want to attract beneficial insects, they're going to need a food source!

This chapter will also take you through how to green up spaces in your wider community and ways to be more sustainable by reusing your garden waste. Gardening in a way that protects and supports the environment has never been more important, so here's how to play your part.

DIY BUG HOTEL

Create a wildlife haven with a few simple materials.

You will need
- 3–4 wooden pallets (these can come in various sizes so choose one that will suit your space)
- Bricks
- Pine cones
- Dried leaves
- Straw
- Shredded pepper
- Wool
- Hollow bamboo canes
- Roofing materials, such as old tiles, roofing felt or tarpaulin
- 1–2 hours

1 First choose your site; you will need an even, firm surface. It can be in a cool and shady spot or a bright and sunny one; you'll attract different species depending on the conditions.

2 Place some bricks under each corner of the first pallet for stability and put the rest of the pallets on top.

3 Once the pallets are stacked, fill the gaps with your chosen materials.

4 To keep your bug hotel reasonably dry, create a 'roof' using some old tiles, roofing felt, tarpaulin, or whatever you have to hand.

5 Share your handiwork on social media; you might inspire others to do the same!

GIVE HEDGEHOGS A HELPING HAND

- Hedgehogs are increasingly reliant on urban and suburban gardens to find the food and shelter they need. You can help them by building homes and making it easier for them to roam between gardens.

- Work with your neighbours to provide access for hedgehogs by making a hole in the bottom section of your fences. Hedgehogs travel quite a long way in search of food, usually over 1.6km (1 mile) a night!

- Have areas where hedgehogs can curl up and get comfortable, such as piles of old leaves or log stacks. This will provide them with plenty of food as well as shelter. Alternatively, build them a home using pieces of plywood nailed together to form a box with a lid, and stuff it with leaves or straw.

- Adopt a hedgehog through your local wildlife trust.

Bird, butterfly and bee friendly

There's a whole host of plants you can grow to attract birds, butterflies, bees and other insects to your space. What's more, many of these plants look great together, so you can create something that not only looks good but does good as well.

BIRDS

Trees and shrubs that produce berries can be a real help to birds over the winter months, as well as providing them with a place to shelter. Plants that produce an abundance of nutrient-rich seeds are an important food source too.

OPPOSITE Blackbird in crab-apple tree; small tortoiseshell butterfly on buddleia.

Bird-friendly plants
The berries on holly, pyracantha and mountain ash are particularly loved by birds.

Crab-apple trees are well suited to a small garden and will give you a long season of interest, with blossom in late spring and small, colourful fruits in autumn. You can cook and eat some of the fruit if you wish – but leave plenty for the birds!

Various shrubs grown on balconies can be a useful resting spot for small birds in cities. Growing in a container can put a bit more stress on a plant as it's solely reliant on you for food and water, and this stress can make them more susceptible to aphids. But be patient and you might find bluetits will hoover them up for you.

Sunflowers left to go to seed will offer an invaluable food source for birds. Once

SUPPORTING WILDLIFE

Plants are one way to encourage wildlife to your garden, but there are other things you can do to support your visitors once they've arrived.

- Think about creating spaces for birds to drink and bathe. This could be as simple as using an empty flowerpot, turning it upside down and gluing a large saucer on top, then filling the saucer with water. If you pop some pebbles in the saucer, this will give the birds somewhere to perch and access for thirsty bees.

- Not all butterflies breed in gardens, but those that do might appreciate nasturtiums, currants, holly or ivy to act as a food source for their larvae.

- Create nesting sites for wild bees by making a bug hotel (see page 150). Bear in mind they may also nest in holes in soil or masonry.

the plants have gone over, leave the flower heads dotted about for birds to find and feast on. They look good grown with asters, teasels and grasses, such as pennisetum, all of which also produce seedheads that are brilliant for birds.

BUTTERFLIES

Flat-topped plants are useful for butterflies to rest on while they feed on the nectar inside the flowers. They are particularly drawn to certain colours, including pink, purple, yellow and orange. Full sun is necessary to attract butterflies, so place your nectar-rich flowering plants in your brightest spots.

Butterfly-friendly plants

Yarrow has tightly clustered flower heads forming a flat top, which allows butterflies to rest while they feed on these nectar-rich plants.

Buddleia, also known by the common name 'butterfly bush', is well known for attracting butterflies. These plants come in a range of hues, from blush pink, lilac and royal blue, or go for the more unusual *Buddleja globosa* with its spherical yellow flower clusters. They can make large shrubs, so for a small space try smaller varieties such as 'High Five Purple' or 'Sugar Plum'.

Echinacea is another plant loved by butterflies and will look beautiful grown in drifts alongside achillea, salvias or grasses.

Sedum is a sun-loving plant that has fleshy leaves tinged with grey, purple or red, and produces flat-topped flower clusters that attract butterflies. They are pretty, compact plants and easy to grow in pots.

BEES

Bees are particularly drawn to plants that are blue or purple as they're able to see these more easily than other colours. Within this colour range is a whole host of plants that look great together and which bees will certainly thank you for.

Bee-friendly plants

Sages come in many wondrous forms, but a hardy ornamental variety such as *Salvia nemorosa* 'Ostfriesland' is one of the best choices to attract bees. These compact plants produce deep purple flower spikes that bees will cling to all summer long. They're easily divided so you can dot them about all over your patch.

Lavender is a well-known favourite for attracting bees. It looks great in pots and will work beautifully on a balcony or patio.

Scabious flowers provide a comfortable spot for a snoozing bee. These plants form evergreen mounds of soft green, sometimes deeply cut foliage, which can be susceptible to mildew, so keep well-watered.

Echium vulgare, otherwise known as viper's bugloss, is a great way to attract bees, and loves a well-drained spot in full sun. Leave the seedheads on over winter to ensure it self-seeds around your patch.

Bee on salvia.

Mini meadow

WHAT ARE MEADOWS AND WHY DO THEY MATTER?

Essentially, a meadow is an area of land consisting of grasses and wild flowers. In the past, this would have been a farmer's field left to grow as it pleases, before being cut for hay in the summer.

With changes in how we grow our food, today meadows are in rapid decline, which is having a direct impact on populations of insects, birds and mammals. You can do your bit to help by growing your own meadow at home, and you don't need a huge area of land to do it. If you do grow your own meadow, you'll be helping to create a wildlife-rich habitat that stores carbon, increases biodiversity and can improve your wellbeing just by looking at it.

A meadow can be created in as little a space as 1 sq. m (11 sq. ft). See step-by-step instructions on the following page.

HOW TO BUY WILDFLOWER SEED

Commercially available seed mixes are an easy way to get your meadow started. Here's what to look out for.

- Use UK-sourced seed.

- Choose a mix that includes perennials as well as annuals; in this way you can have plants coming up year after year.

- Try to avoid mixes that contain non-native species as these can become invasive and threaten native wild flowers.

1 Choose an open, sunny spot. Remove any problem plants such as docks, nettles or brambles.

2 Dig over the patch of ground you're turning into a meadow, firm it down by treading on it back and forth, then rake it over to create a soil texture that is light and crumbly.

3 Let the soil settle for a few weeks and hoe off or fork out any weed seeds that germinate.

4 Sow your meadow-seed mix in spring or early autumn. Sow it in two different directions using a wrist-flicking motion to scatter it, then firm it down with the back of a rake.

5 Water the seed in. You may need to water again if it hasn't rained after a week.

6 You may need to protect the seed from birds. You can use netting or tie some string across your meadow area, and recycle your old CDs by hanging them from the string.

7 Once the meadow has finished flowering in late summer, cut it with a mower and remove the clippings. This will help keep the fertility in the soil low and ensure wild flowers are better able to establish.

MAKING SEED BOMBS

If you want to brighten up different corners of your garden, a fun way to do this is by making seed bombs. These little balls of compacted clay and seed are cheap and easy to make, and you'll have fun seeing what pops up!

You will need
- 1 packet of wildflower seed mix
- 250g of powdered clay
- 625g of peat-free multipurpose compost
- Water
- Mixing bowl
- 1–2 hours

1 In the bowl, mix together your seed mix, powdered clay and compost.

2 Add water a little at a time until it all starts to stick together.

3 Roll the mixture into balls between the palms of your hands.

4 Leave the seed bombs to dry somewhere sunny.

5 Once they're dry, throw them, break them up or dig them into bare soil and enjoy seeing what comes up.

Community gardening

Community gardens are a rich, local resource that not only have benefits for wildlife but also for the people that look after them. Getting involved in one is a great way to meet like-minded people and to learn, as well as contributing to something that is benefiting your local area.

Each community garden may have a different focus, from creating food-growing areas to wildlife conservation, but one thing they all have in common is that they make a big difference.

WHY GET INVOLVED?

• If you don't have access to outside space, joining a community garden means you can still have all the benefits of looking after plants, while helping others at the same time.

• You'll definitely improve your horticultural knowledge and skills.

• Community gardens are a good way to regenerate an area and make it a nicer place to be.

• Stress and anxiety levels can be significantly reduced due to the time spent outside taking care of a green space.

HOW TO GET INVOLVED

An easy way to get involved is to join an existing group in your local area. The RHS has a list of community gardening groups on its website, including Britain in Bloom associations. Some community groups may advertise for volunteers on social media or local bulletin boards. Alternatively, you might want to set one up yourself. If so, there are a few things you'll need to consider.

- Look for a suitable location and ask the landowner's permission to start your project. You'll need to organise some public liability insurance to protect you or your group in case of accidents and any other issues.

- Get as many volunteers involved as you can by contacting schools and nurseries, local businesses or other community groups. You can then work together to decide what sort of garden you want to create in a way that best represents your community. This might be using the space as a food-growing area, wildlife conservation, a wellbeing garden or a memorial garden.

- Fundraise, fundraise, fundraise. Some local businesses or charities may be willing to donate resources, and you could ask for help and advice from local gardeners.

- Have a good look around your site. As well as working out your aspect and soil type, think about any features you can keep, such as mature trees, existing planting or pathways.

- Keep sustainability in mind when designing your garden by making space for compost heaps and water butts, and re-purposing materials such as pallets, guttering, even old tyres stacked up to make plant containers.

BRING IT TO LIFE

If you're embarking on creating your own community garden, here are some top tips to help you look after your space.

- Consider who will take care of your plants on a day-to-day basis. If you're enlisting the help of volunteers, think about drawing up a rota to make sure things get watered regularly.

- Right plant, right place. Choose plants that will be suitable for your site and will tolerate your soil conditions. Perennials are often a cost-effective and sustainable option.

- Could you go organic? Cutting out the use of chemicals is not only better for the environment but safer for everyone using your garden.

- Keep your paths clear and remove any low-hanging or problematic branches from trees and shrubs that could make access tricky.

Composting

As well as reducing the amount of waste that goes to landfill, composting is an excellent way to incorporate goodness back into your soil.

As discussed in Chapter 1, adding organic matter, whether that's composted food, plant waste or well-rotted manure, all helps to improve the structure of your soil. This means it can hold on to water and nutrients more easily. As the organic matter breaks down, nutrients are released slowly over time, keeping your plants healthy and happy.

There are different techniques available, whether you have an allotment, back garden or no outdoor space, and all have slightly different requirements for successful composting.

BOKASHI

From the Japanese meaning 'fermented organic matter', Bokashi composting is an anaerobic process in which food waste, including dairy, cooked food and meat, is fermented using microorganisms (usually a mixture of bacteria, yeast and fungi). These are incorporated into a special 'bran' that you spread over the surface of the food in a lidded container.

- You can buy Bokashi kits (consisting of two containers and the bran) online; some local authorities may provide them at a discount.

- Unlike normal composting, you need to eliminate air as much as possible by squashing the food waste down each time you top up the bin, and keep the lid firmly in place.

- Make sure the food waste is chopped up small and add some bran after each layer of food is added.

- Every couple of days, drain off the liquid that forms using the tap at the bottom and use this diluted with water as a plant feed.

- When one bucket is full, start on the second.

- After a couple of weeks, a white mould may appear on the food in the first bin, and it will be ready for emptying. White mould is fine but green is bad and is usually a sign of not enough bran or too much air.

- It should smell a bit like vinegar, and you may still be able to identify some of the food you put in. This is normal and it will break down eventually once it's being used in the garden.

- Fermented waste can be dug into the soil, mixed with old compost from grow bags or to top dress containers. Adding in thin layers rather than clumps will help it break down more quickly once it's been incorporated into your soil or old compost. It can also be quite acidic so if you want to add some to a wormery, do so in small quantities and add plenty of crushed eggshells to neutralise some of the acidity.

WORMERY

Worm composting is an efficient way to turn kitchen waste and small amounts of garden waste into compost and concentrated liquid fertiliser.

- You can either buy a ready-made kit or make your own, which can be cheaper.

- Ready-made kits usually have several layers of trays stacked together containing live worms. The worms munch through the kitchen waste, with the finished compost collecting at the bottom. The advantage of a kit is that it is easier to use the compost without having to separate the worms out first.

DIY WORMERY

Here is a simple way to make your own wormery.

You will need
- Large plastic box with a lid (an old recycling box works well)
- Drill
- Bricks or wooden blocks
- Newspaper
- Peat-free compost or coir
- Suitable worm species (from a friend's wormery or buy online)
- 30 minutes–1 hour

1 The worms will need air so drill lots of holes in the base of the box, and a few near the top too.

2 Sit the box on bricks, wooden blocks or anything you have to hand to act as 'feet', which will allow air to circulate around it.

3 Cover the bottom with a few sheets of newspaper.

4 Add a good layer of moist, peat-free compost or coir on top of the newspaper. This acts as 'bedding' for your worms and is what they will live in while they're busy digesting your food waste.

5 Add your worms. These can be bought online and may be sold as 'Tiger worms' or Dendrobaena worms. They are the most suitable, as earthworms from the garden won't do the job. You will need about 400–500 worms to start your wormery.

6 Give them a small amount of chopped-up food waste to start off with. Add shredded paper or cardboard occasionally too for a good balance.

7 Cover with damp newspaper or cardboard and put the lid on. Worms like it dark and damp so remember: moisture in, light out. Feed them little and often.

- As well as compost (known as vermicompost), a liquid is also produced that you can use diluted as plant food.

- An ideal place to site your wormery is somewhere dry and shady with good ventilation. You should add food waste little and often, and ideally chopped up to make it easier for the worms to break it down further.

- You can keep a wormery in your kitchen, but if you add too much food at once the worms won't be able to digest it all, leading to smells. Wait until the worms have digested the top layer of waste before adding more.

- They'll eat raw or cooked veg, teabags, eggshells, coffee grounds, small amounts of citrus peel, shredded paper and cardboard. Try to avoid oily or spicy food waste.

TRADITIONAL COMPOSTING

Typically, composting involves breaking down kitchen and garden waste outside in a large container or heap. The decomposition occurs because of naturally occurring bacteria and fungi. Small invertebrates, such as composting worms and millipedes, help to complete the process.

- Compost bins come in a range of sizes to fit most spaces. Site somewhere shady and ideally sit it on top of the earth or add a spadeful of soil to the bottom of the bin.

- Alternatively, an open heap can be made using pallets or fence panels to create 2–3 compartments, one for fresh material and another to turn it into.

- Turning helps to incorporate oxygen, which will help the material break down more quickly. It can take about 6–12 months for it to be usable as garden compost.

- You ideally need a 50:50 mix of material that's high in nitrogen (such as grass clippings, herbaceous material) and carbon (such as woody prunings from shrubs, paper, cardboard, dead leaves). Too much of one or the other can lead to a slimy, smelly mess.

Watering a compost heap helps microorganisms break down organic waste.

- Once one compartment is full you can turn it over into the next, until eventually the material has broken down enough to use as compost. If you have just one compost bin, turn over what's inside with a garden fork.

- Do not add meat, fish, dairy, etc. as this can encourage rodents.

WAYS TO USE YOUR COMPOST AND LIQUID FERTILISER

- Dilute liquid fertiliser from your wormery or bokashi bin with water (1:10 or 1:20 for a bokashi) and use as a liquid feed for your container plants or particularly hungry veg, such as squashes, peppers and tomatoes.

- Use your compost as a mulch. Spread this in autumn, winter or spring to lock in moisture, suppress weeds and improve your soil structure.

- Add compost to potting mixes when planting up containers.

- Top dress your container plants in spring with compost for a boost just before the growing season gets going.

- Mix into beds or planting holes before planting out.

8. Plant Clinic

It's important to accept that occasionally during your plant-care journey things might go wrong from time to time. You will almost certainly kill one or two. While this is obviously not your aim, it's an all-important part of learning how to garden. Even the most experienced plant experts get things wrong sometimes, so don't be too hard on yourself if you have a sad-looking houseplant or seeds that just won't germinate.

This chapter will take you through some of the key things you need to know when looking after plants, particularly those in pots. The main thing to remember is not to be daunted, just have a go. After all, you can always try again.

Watering

Plants need a good balance of air and water in the soil they're planted in. This is crucial in helping them take up the nutrients they need through their roots.

If the soil or compost is moist then this will help the plants stay healthy, but if there's too much water, air is pushed out. This is bad news for most plants, as not having enough air leads to a build-up of toxins and a very poorly plant. On the other hand, too much air and not enough moisture can lead to wilting and weak growth.

It's important to get this balance right by watering carefully, and only when you need to. Here's what to look out for.

Signs of underwatering
- Newest growth at the tips is weak and floppy.
- Soil is completely dried out.
- Pot feels light when picked up.

Signs of overwatering
- More mature growth is weak and floppy, as well as new growth at the tips.
- Soil is wet all the way down inside the pot.
- Pot feels very heavy when picked up.
- Overwatering is difficult to recover from so try to avoid it if you can, especially in winter when plant growth slows down.

Just right
- Plant looks perky and healthy.
- There is some moisture visible in the compost, perhaps a few centimetres below the surface.

WHY IS MY PLANT …

… going yellow?

There can be a few different things going on here. An issue with watering could be the culprit. If your plant is in a pot, check the compost to see if it's too wet or too dry. Your plant could be hungry, so try a high nitrogen feed once a week. It's also possible that your plant may be getting too much or not enough light. Remember, though, that sometimes leaves yellow as part of the natural aging and shedding process.

… not flowering?

This could be due to light levels. Although some plants are more tolerant of low light levels than others, not enough light will cause flowering to stop. It's worth remembering that flowering also requires a lot of energy. Your plant may be in a resting phase until it's ready to flower again.

… not growing?

Some plants are slow to put on a lot of growth, perhaps just gaining a few millimetres a year. Make sure you're providing the right light and moisture levels, and feed once a week through the growing season.

… going brown at the tips?

This is likely to be an issue around humidity and can particularly affect houseplants. Increase humidity by misting, grouping plants together or standing them in trays of pebbles topped up with water. It's worth checking the compost if your plant is in a pot just in case there is an issue with over- or underwatering too.

HOW TO WATER

There are a few different techniques you can try when watering your plants to help give them what they need without overdoing it. If one method isn't working for you, try another; it's always good to experiment.

Watering from above

- Use your watering can or hose to moisten the compost by aiming for the roots rather than the leaves. This technique works well when watering plants in the ground or those in medium to large containers.
- A rose attachment with small holes for use with a watering can will produce smaller water droplets, and this is useful when watering seedlings.
- Using a rose attachment distributes water evenly and avoids flooding a plant with water too quickly.

Watering from below

- Submerging a plant pot in a bucket or tub with a few centimetres of water is a good way to avoid overwatering, as the plant takes up what it needs. It is easy to see the compost darkening near the surface when it's had enough.
- Smaller houseplants and succulents may benefit from this type of watering. This will help you avoid scorch marks from light hitting water droplets sitting on the leaves, or leaves rotting from getting too wet when watered from overhead.

Feeding

Getting this right is key for maximising plant growth and health, so here is what you need to know.

When?

- It's best to feed plants when they're actively growing. This will happen as light levels and temperatures start to increase, from spring onwards. There are many different plant feeds on the market and they all contain a mix of the most important nutrients: nitrogen, potassium and phosphorous.

How?

- Liquid feeds tend to be faster acting, as the plant can take up the nutrients it wants immediately. You can try soluble powders, or liquid feeds diluted in water, such as seaweed. Many liquid feeds often include 'micronutrients' that help support plant growth and make them more resistant to stress.

- You can also add granulated feeds to compost before planting into containers. These gradually break down and feed the plant slowly over time.

- Always follow the dosage instructions whichever feed you use. Overfeeding can cause lots of weak, floppy growth which is more susceptible to pests and other problems. It's better to feed the right amount on a regular basis.

Dos and don'ts when feeding

Do feed and water in cooler parts of the day, i.e., early morning and late evening. Unless using a feed specifically designed for the purpose, try to avoid splashing foliage with liquid feed as this can cause scorching.

Don't feed in cooler months of the year. Growth will have slowed down and you may end up with a plant with new growth that could be damaged by frosts. You'll know this has happened if you see blackened leaves and stems.

GROW YOUR OWN PLANT FOOD

If you have a spare corner in your growing space, try growing your own plant food.

Comfrey is an attractive plant with nodding, bell-shaped flowers in pink, purple or blue, usually growing best in full sun but coping well in partial shade. Its best quality is its incredibly nutritious leaves, full of nitrogen, potassium and phosphorous.

You can make your own plant food from comfrey in two ways.

Liquid feed

1 Cut leaves from the plant, but wear gloves as the hairs on the leaves can irritate the skin.

2 Fill a bucket with water and put the leaves in, making sure they are covered with water.

3 Cover the bucket. After 4–6 weeks you will have an incredibly smelly (but nutritious) liquid feed. Strain off the debris (you can compost this) and use your feed on hungry plants like squashes and tomatoes, with no need to dilute.

Concentrated feed

1 You will need a couple of plastic, 1-litre drink bottles: one to use as a collecting vessel, and the other to hold the comfrey leaves as they break down.

2 Cut off the bottom of one of the bottles, and pack in plenty of comfrey leaves. Cover the end with a plastic bag to prevent drying out and secure with an elastic band.

3 Wedge this bottle upside down so it's connected to your collecting vessel. As the leaves rot, a brown liquid will drip down. You'll need to dilute this with about 1 part feed to 20 parts water.

Diseases

The best way to keep your plants healthy is to give them the growing conditions that suit them best. Good garden hygiene is also important, such as clearing away dead material and disinfecting tools and boots, especially after you have been pruning or digging out a sick plant. Try to stick to a regular feeding and watering regime, and give plants space to encourage good air flow.

Despite all this, factors outside your control, such as the weather, can have an impact on the health and vigour of your plants.

There are also many different types of diseases that can affect plants, often caused by bacteria or viruses. The ones that occur most commonly, however, are due to fungal problems, which are especially prevalent if plants get stressed in dry conditions or if the weather is warm and wet.

I've got ... Grey fuzzy mould appearing on fruits, leaves and flowers.

This sounds like ... A common fungal problem known as grey mould or botrytis. It often appears in warm, damp conditions.

What should I do? Ensure good air flow between plants and water at the base. Remove dead and dying plants straight away, and improve ventilation if growing in a greenhouse.

I've got ... A white, dusty looking coating on the leaves.

This sounds like ... Powdery mildew, which can affect lots of ornamental plants and veg.

What should I do? Water regularly to avoid your plants becoming limp in hot weather. Destroy infected leaves and make sure there's good air circulation between plants.

I've got ... Round black spots on the leaves; leaves are yellowing and dropping off.

This sounds like ... Black spot, a fungal disease that is common on roses but can affect other flowers and fruit too. It's not fatal but can weaken your plant over time.

What should I do? Mulch well and water at the roots. You can spray on fungicide, but this requires regular application to be effective. Garlic spray can also be effective, sprayed at weekly intervals. Clear away infected leaves in autumn to try to break the cycle.

I've got ... A black, fuzzy mould on the stems and leaves; leaves are dropping off.

This sounds like ... Sooty mould, often caused by aphids. Aphids leave behind sticky secretions, which allow this black mould to grow. It will weaken your plant by reducing the effectiveness of photosynthesis.

What should I do? Clean sooty mould off leaves if possible. Discourage aphids with a weekly spray of garlic, or an organic insecticide. Companion planting that attracts aphid predators such as hoverflies and ladybirds may also help; try pot marigolds, garlic chives or French marigolds.

I've got ... Orange spots on the stems and leaves.

This sounds like ... Rust. The orange spots often appear in damp weather and can affect a range of plants, including garlic, onions, pear trees, hollyhocks and daylilies.

What should I do? Destroy infected leaves or whole plants so the fungal spores can't spread or overwinter. If it is on your veg, it won't affect the taste but will just make them look less attractive.

When disposing of plant material that's affected by fungal problems, you can burn or bury it. Composting through council environmental waste schemes is also an option as these facilities will reach high enough temperatures to kill off most diseases. Less persistent diseases, such as rust or mildew, can be composted at home if you've managed to catch them early.

Pests

Coming across pests is an inevitable part of gardening and doesn't always have to spell disaster. It's a good idea to try to tolerate them up to a point as their presence will eventually encourage predators to do all the hard work for you. Having pests present in high numbers, however, will be detrimental to your plants and affect their overall vigour. Here's a guide to some of the most common and how to deal with them.

Vine weevil.

VINE WEEVIL

These are a very common pest when plants are grown in pots and can be tricky to shift. Adult beetles are dark brown-black in colour and their presence can be detected when notches appear on the outside edges of leaves. The grubs, though, are more of a problem. These small, C-shaped white creatures feed on the roots of plants over autumn and winter, leading to wilting and death.

What to do about them
- Re-pot plants regularly if possible. This will give you a chance to inspect the compost for grubs.
- Adults can be caught using sticky traps placed around the edges of pots.
- A biological control called a nematode can be applied, usually in the form of a powder. These microscopic predatory worms seek out the grubs and kill them.

MEALY BUG

These sap-sucking insects are common on houseplants and thrive in warm, dry conditions. Their presence can often be detected when sticky, fluffy white masses appear under leaves or on stems. Underneath this are the insects and/or their eggs.

What to do about them

- If you have a very heavy infestation, it may be better to dispose of the plant completely.
- Biological controls, such as predatory ladybirds and parasitic wasps, are available but are expensive and tend to work best in large greenhouses.
- Mealy bugs and their eggs can be wiped off. Use a damp cotton bud to reach tricky areas.

APHIDS

These rather annoying insects can reproduce quickly in warm weather and will weaken plants, causing growth to look distorted. Their sticky secretions (known as honeydew) can encourage sooty mould to form.

What to do about them
- Try weekly applications of an organic insecticide.
- Attract predators, including ladybirds and hoverflies, with suitable companion plants.
- Try growing pot marigolds, sunflowers or strongly scented plants such as garlic chives and curry plants.

SPIDER MITE

Tiny and sap-sucking, these insects love warm and dry conditions. Like aphids, they will often gather on the underside of leaves. Mites are a yellow-green colour, but sometimes appear red later in the year. Affected plants will have leaves with a speckled appearance on the upper surface, and a fine webbing may be visible on plants with a heavy infestation.

What to do about them
- Raise humidity levels by misting house plants or sitting them on pebble-filled trays topped up with water.
- If you have a greenhouse, then 'damp down' on warm days by watering the floor and staging, and ensure good ventilation.
- If using an organic insecticide, be sure to wet the underside of the leaves where the mites will be hiding.

SLUGS AND SNAILS

These creatures do actually have an important role to play in helping to aerate soil and by eating away decaying matter. However, they can also be horribly destructive, especially when tasty young seedlings or salad crops are available. You may notice shiny trails that show where they've been, or nibbled edges on plant leaves.

What to do about them

- Slugs and snails often don't like the sharp texture of crushed eggshells or grit, so add a layer of either of these around plants that might be susceptible.
- Use citrus fruit to trap them. Cut an orange or grapefruit in half and scoop out the insides. Place the empty halves outside (cut side down) near any vulnerable plants for the slugs to investigate. You can compost the spent rinds.
- Organic slug pellets may be worth a try.

BENEFICIAL BUGS

Sharing your growing space with living things is important for a healthy garden. There are lots of helpful insects that will act as pollinators and increase your veg crop, while their larvae will do the job of tackling pests for you. Provide cosy spots for bugs to overwinter and plenty of flowering plants to encourage adults to visit and lay eggs. Here are some garden heroes to look out for in your outdoor space.

Ladybirds
Feed on aphids and sometimes scale insects. Larvae are grey/black with orange or white markings. Often overwinter in leaf and log piles.

Green lacewings
The larvae gobble up aphids and other insects. Adults have pale-green bodies with transparent wings and like hibernating in evergreen shrubs. Adults feed on nectar, honeydew and pollen, so provide lots of flowering plants for them.

Hoverflies

These yellow- and black-striped insects dart about with a characteristic hover in mid-flight. Adults act as pollinators and have a diet similar to lacewings. The larvae are ferocious eaters of aphids.

Earwigs

These eat some plant material and other insects. Useful on fruit trees for eating fruit aphids, but without damaging the tree or the fruit.

Glossary

Annual A plant that completes its life cycle within one year, then dies.

Biennial A plant that completes its life cycle within two years, then dies. In its first year there will be leafy growth, followed by flowers in the second year.

Deadheading A process where old flower heads are removed, usually before they've gone to seed. This encourages new flowers to form.

Deciduous Trees and some shrubs that lose their leaves during autumn.

Evergreen Trees and some shrubs that keep their leaves all year round; some older leaves may be shed from time to time.

Garden compost Used to fertilise and improve soil. Usually made from a mixture of plant and food waste that has decomposed over time. Different from potting compost, which is specially formulated for plants to grow in.

Germination The stage at which a plant develops from a seed or spore after being dormant for a period of time.

Hardy Able to withstand temperatures that fall to freezing or below.

Half hardy Able to withstand cold temperatures for a period of time, but unlikely to withstand freezing.

Micronutrient A chemical element needed in tiny amounts to support healthy growth.

Misting Spraying a fine cloud of water droplets over plants to increase humidity.

Mulch A covering placed on the surface of the soil. This can include manure, bark or garden compost, gravel, pebbles or even a permeable membrane.

Organic matter Material that is of plant or animal origin. This includes manures and garden composts used to enrich the soil.

Perennial A plant that will live for several years.

Photosynthesis A process used by plants to convert light energy into chemical energy, which fuels growth and reproduction.

Pollinator An animal that moves pollen from the male parts of a flower to the female parts.

Propagator Used to incubate seeds at a set temperature in order to encourage germination.

Pumice A light and porous volcanic rock that can be used to top dress containers or terrariums for a neater finish.

Succulent Plants, such as aloe vera, with thick, fleshy leaves that hold on to water.

Thinning Where excess numbers of seedlings are removed so remaining plants have enough space to grow.

Variegated Plants with leaves that have different-coloured edges or patterns.

Wilting Where a plant becomes limp through too much heat, not enough water or disease.

Index

air plants 108
allium 48, 92
aloe vera 69, 109
amaranth 40
Amelanchier 98
annual mallow 86
annuals 36–8, 85–6, 88–9
anxiety 69
aphids 183
areca palm 119
aspects in gardens 15
aster 92
Astrantias 14

balcony gardening 10, 54
bamboo 53, 84
basil 39, 61, 63, 128, 129, 134, 139
bathroom plants 116–18
bedroom plants 119–21
bee-friendly plants 156
beetroot 134
beneficial bugs 184–5
bergamot 58
biennials 90
bird feeders 78
bird-friendly plants 152, 155
black spot 179
blackberries 55
blackcurrants 147
Bokashi 164–6
borage 131, 139
Boston fern 118
bouquets 96–7

bromeliad 118
brunnera 53
budding plants 18
buddleia 14, 155–6
bug hotel 150, 154
bulbs 48–51, 54
bunny tails 86
butterfly-friendly plants 155–6
buying plants 17–18

calibrachoa 39
calming scents 58, 60
carex 42, 53
carrot 145
catmint 42
chamomile 60, 68, 130
chard 55
cherry 98
chilli plants 39, 141, 145
Chinese evergreen 120
Chinese money plant 121
chives 55, 129, 132, 139
chocolate cosmos 65
choisya 42, 43
Christmas box 79
Christmas wreath 100–1
citrus 61
clay soil 12, 14
climbers 44–7
cocktails & mocktails
  grapefruit and ginger spritzer 73
  lavender martini 72

minty summer spritz 70
  rose sangria 72
  rosemary and orange refresher 73
  thyme lemonade 74
comfrey 176
community gardening 161–3
companion planting 130–1
composting 14, 84, 164–9
compost bags 20
container gardening
  bulbs 51
  choosing pots 32–3
  cut flowers 84, 86–7
  edible plants 39, 55, 142–3
  feeds for 33
  houseplants 104
  planting in 20
  succulents 35
  watering 33
coriander 39, 132, 134
cornus 43, 69, 92, 98
cosmos 36, 65, 92
coughs and colds 66
courgette 143
crab apple 14, 152
crocus 48, 92
curry plant 131
cut flowers
  annuals 85–6, 88–9
  arrangements 89
  biennials 90
  bouquets 96–7

containers for 84, 86–7
creating 82–4
dried flowers 98
foraging for 99–101
perennials 91
picking method 94–5
seasonal picks 92
stems 98
cuts and scrapes 69
cyclamen 69

daffodil 92
dahlia 92
deadheading 33
devil's ivy 113
dianthus 92
dibbers 24
dill 86, 92, 139
diseases 178–80
division 43
dragon tree 114
dried flowers 98
dwarf iris 49

earwigs 185
east-facing gardens 15
Ebers Papyrus 69
echinacea 41, 156
edible flowers 137–9
euonymus 39
euphorbia 92
evergreen plants 39

fargesia 42
fatsia 43
feeds 33, 105, 175–6
fennel 55, 134, 139
ferns 53, 54

fescues 42–3
fiddle-leaf fig 113
floral tape 95
flower arranging 89
flower scissors 95
flowering perennials 41–2
foliage 53, 85, 88
foliage stripper 95
foraging 99–101
fork 28
foxgloves 54, 90
French beans 143, 145
fruit trees 55
fuchsia 14

garlic 66, 141
gazania 36, 37
giant oat grass 91
ginger 59, 61, 66, 67, 73
globe thistle 91
gloves 27
goji berries 147
grape hyacinth 48, 54
grapefruit and ginger
   spritzer 73
grasses 42–3, 53
green lacewing 184
grey mould 178
ground rake 28

hakon grass 42
hand forks 27
hand trowels 27
hardy geraniums 14, 41, 54
hare's ear 86
hazel 98
headaches 68
hedgehogs 151

helenium 91, 92
heliotrope 65
hellebore 14, 77, 92
herbs 55, 128–32, 145
heucheras 53
hoe 28
holly 152, 154
home remedies
   anxiety 69
   coughs and colds 66
   cuts and scrapes 69
   headaches 68
   nausea 67
   sleep 68
honesty 90
honeysuckle 64
honeywort 85, 86
hops 60
houseplants 10
   bathroom 116–18
   bedroom 119–21
   choosing 100
   dos and don'ts 105
   kokodama 110–11
   living room 112–14
   marimo moss balls 115
   style tips 106–8
   terrariums 123–5
   in winter 122
hoverflies 185
hyacinth 92
hydrangea 91

imperial fritillary 49
inch plant 118
ivy 39, 44, 99, 106, 110–11,
   112, 154

jade plant 109
Japanese maple 14
Jekyll, Gertrude 6

kale 55, 143, 145
kneeler 28
kohl rabi 142, 145
kokodama 110–11

lady palm 120
ladybirds 184
lamb's lettuce 134
lavender 58, 60, 69, 72, 137, 156
lavender martini 72
lemon balm 61
lemon verbena 130
lettuce 145
lilac 92
lily 48–9, 54, 92
living room plants 112–14
lobelia 39
loppers 28

magnolia 92
mahonia 65
mangetout 143
manure 14, 84
marimo moss balls 115
marjoram 55
meadows 157–8
mealy bug 182
Mexican sunflower 38
microgreens 134–5
mint 55, 70, 75, 129, 132
mint limeade 75
minty summer spritz 70

mizuna 55, 134
mood boosting scents 61–2
mountain ash 152
mustard 55, 133

narcissus 49
nasturtium 69, 139, 154
nausea 67
north-facing gardens 15

old man's beard 99
onions 143
oregano 130

pansies 137
parsley 55, 131, 132
parsnip 145
peace lily 113
peat 13
penstemon 92
peony 92
pepper plants 39, 142
peppermint 58, 60, 67
perennials
  cut flowers 91
  division 43
  flowering 41–2
  grasses 42–3
  planting 21
  shrubs 43
pests 18, 181–4
planting
  bulbs 51
  climbers 46–7
  perennials 21
  shrubs 21
  time for 20

trees 21
  weeding 20
plug plants 38–9
polka dot begonia 114
poppy 92
pot marigold 36, 131, 139
powdery mildew 179
prayer plant 106
pricking out 24
pruning saw 28
purple vervain 88
pussy willow 98
pyracantha 152

radicchio 55
radish 142, 145
raised beds 143
raspberries 75, 146
raspberry rose fizz 75
redcurrants 55
rhubarb 146
rocket 55, 134
rose 62, 63, 71, 75, 92, 137
rose sangria 71
rosemary 39, 61, 68, 73, 91, 130
rosemary and orange refresher 73
rosewater 63, 75
rosularia 35
rotating 141
rowan 14
rudbeckia 88–9
rust 180

sage 37, 38, 39, 156
salad leaves 133–5

sandy soil 12
scabious 37, 38, 85, 156
scented plants
  for calm 58, 60
  garden plants 62, 64–5
  for mood boost 61–2
sea holly 90
secateurs 27
sedges 53
sedum 35, 156
seed bomb 159
seeds 46, 22–5, 157
sempervivum 35
shade 52–5, 131, 173
shrubs 21, 43, 152
shungiku 134
size of plants 18
sleep 68
slugs 184
snails 184
snake plant 116
snapdragon 88, 92
snowdrop 49, 79
soil types 12–14
sooty mould 180
south-facing gardens 15
sowing seeds 22–5
spade 28
spider flower 89
spider mite 183
spider plant 116
spinach 134
square metre veg plot
  144–5
star jasmine 64
stems 98, 100–1
stocks 62

straw flower 38
strawberries 71, 147
string of pearls 106
succulents 35, 109
sugar flowers 138
summer savory 130
sunflower 37, 38, 92, 152,
  155
support wire 95
swede 145
sweet alyssum 64
sweet peas 64–5, 86
sweet william 90
Swiss chard 143

tatsoi 134
terrariums 123–5
thinning out 25
thyme 39, 74, 128
thyme lemonade 74
Tibetan cherry 69
tomato plants 39, 142, 145
trailing plants 39
trees 21, 54
trellis 45
trug 28
tulip 48, 49, 92
Turk's cap lilies 54
turnips 145
twine 95

viburnum 14, 43, 79, 92, 98
vine weevil 181
violas 137
viper's bugloss 156

Ward, Nathaniel Bagshaw
  124
watering 33, 109, 172, 173,
  174
watering can 28
weeding 20
west-facing gardens 15
wigwams 44, 45
wildflower seeds 157
willow 92
window boxes 10, 54, 141–2
winter plants 77–9, 122
wintersweet 77
witch hazel 92
woodland gardens 54
wormery 166–8

yarrow 41–2, 155

zinnia 36, 92
ZZ plant 106, 114

Picture Credits

All illustrations are © Patti Blau.

All photographs are © Shutterstock, except for the following:

© GAP Photos: 13 middle and bottom, 82, 93, 94, 96, 158, 163, 174.

© National Trust Images/Chris Lacey: 18.

© Alamy: 46 right, 50, 55, 66, 115, 123, 139 right, 162 right.

© Getty Images: 164.